Peter R Earling

Whom to Trust

Peter R Earling

Whom to Trust

ISBN/EAN: 9783337365936

Printed in Europe, USA, Canada, Australia, Japan

Cover: Foto ©Suzi / pixelio.de

More available books at **www.hansebooks.com**

WHOM TO TRUST:

A PRACTICAL TREATISE

ON

MERCANTILE CREDITS.

By P. R. EARLING,
OF L. GOULD & CO.,
CHICAGO.

CHICAGO AND NEW YORK:
RAND, MCNALLY & COMPANY, PUBLISHERS.
1890.

COPYRIGHT, 1889, BY RAND, McNALLY & CO.

Trust.

THIS TREATISE IS DEDICATED
BY THE AUTHOR,
TO HIS FRIENDS AND ASSOCIATES IN BUSINESS,
L. GOULD AND FRANK GOULD,
AS EMBODYING THE PRINCIPLES AND METHODS ADOPTED
AND UNIFORMLY ADHERED TO BY THEM, THROUGH-
OUT A LONG AND SUCCESSFUL BUSINESS CAREER.

CONTENTS.

INTRODUCTORY.

	PAGE.
INTRODUCTION	11
WHOM IT CONCERNS	15
THE IMPORTANCE OF A KNOWLEDGE OF CREDITS	18
LOSSES BY FAILURES	23
MERCANTILE REPORTS	29

ANALYTICAL.

ANALYSIS OF STATEMENTS OR REPORTS	34
NATURE OF THE BUSINESS	41
LOCALITY	45
CHARACTER AND HABITS	52
ABILITY	55
EXPERIENCE	60
APPLICATION AND INDUSTRY	64
BUSINESS EDUCATION	68
HONESTY	72
ECONOMY	77
MARRIED OR SINGLE	83
AGE	86
CAPITAL	89
ASSETS: STOCK AND PERSONAL PROPERTY	94
ASSETS: ACCOUNTS AND BILLS RECEIVABLE	98
REAL ESTATE—EXEMPTIONS	103
LIABILITIES	106
VOLUME OF BUSINESS IN PROPORTION TO CAPITAL	110
ANTECEDENTS	115
COMPETITION	118

CONTENTS.

	PAGE.
PUNCTUALITY	122
PRODUCTIVE OR NON-PRODUCTIVE	127
DOING BUSINESS AS AGENTS	130
PARTNERSHIPS	134
DOUBTFUL CREDITS	139
JOINT-STOCK AND COÖPERATIVE ASSOCIATIONS	142
WOMEN IN TRADE	148
CHATTEL MORTGAGES AND OTHER LIENS	153
INSURANCE	157
MISCELLANEOUS INFORMATION	161
OLD CUSTOMERS	167
LIMIT OF CREDIT	171
MERCANTILE REPORTS ANALYZED	174
CREDIT: A RISK	200

FACTS IN GENERAL.

INVENTORY VALUATIONS	202
PAST-DUE ACCOUNTS	209
COLLECTIONS	215
COLLECTIONS: METHODS EMPLOYED	220
SHARP COLLECTORS	224
REFERENCES	228
COMMERCIAL TRAVELERS	236
PERSONAL INTERVIEWS VS. REPORTS	241
CHRONIC BORROWERS	244
DEBT VS INDEPENDENCE	248
COMPROMISES AND EXTENSIONS	254
CREDIT: HISTORY OF	260
CREDIT SYSTEM	268
CREDIT: ITS RELATION TO CAPITAL AND LABOR	281
HISTORY OF THE MERCANTILE AGENCY	295

INTRODUCTION.

This treatise on "Mercantile Credits" is the outgrowth of frequent requests on the part of business friends of the writer to give them the benefit of his experience "in making credits," so far, at least, as that might be possible in a very condensed form, and by laying down and illustrating a few fundamental principles. An analysis, however, of the subject showed that a few off-hand rules and directions on "when and when not to make credits" would be inadequate, if not quite useless, since in no two applications for credit are the conditions the same. In the attempt, then, to be of service even to a few personal friends, it was found necessary to treat the subject in a comprehensive manner, and although this involved the systematic and consecutive arrangement and assimilation of a vast quantity of material, and a close scrutiny of its relationship, the task was, nevertheless, deemed worthy the effort.

No apology for presenting this volume to the public is offered. But several valid reasons can be pointed out for its publication. The first reason is, that a better knowledge than is generally possessed of this subject is of the utmost importance to the business interests of the country at large and to individual welfare in particular. Secondly, the total absence of literature and lack of information on a topic of such vital importance to every man engaged in business, would seem to justify an effort to supply so palpable a deficiency. Thirdly, that the experience and knowledge of one who has devoted a life-time to the management of "credits" in both mercantile and manufacturing business, can hardly fail of being beneficial, when made available to those less practiced in this special vocation.

The principles and rules laid down in the following pages for determining credit are such as have governed the writer in his own practice. Close observation of causes, and their natural and probable effects, has made it possible to establish certain standards, more or less fixed, for our guidance in all departments of business.

No new system or better methods than those used by many other credit managers is claimed. In the absence, as we have said, of any published work, the aim has been simply to give the conclusions of a long and active experience, in the best and most intelligible manner possible to the writer. As the "proof of the pudding is in the eating," the merit of the rules here given may be fairly judged by the results obtained in their daily application; and these, were it permissible to give them, would be a sufficient indorsement. This much may be said, that the percentage of losses sustained by houses in general is by far too large, and that a better understanding of the "Science of Credits" would inure largely to the benefit of the business community and save it millions of dollars annually.

The subject-matter has been strictly confined to the text, viz.: Credits. Every chapter has been prepared with special reference to that topic only; but, incidentally, the treatise will be found to cover the fundamental principles underlying business in general, by pointing out the causes that lead to success or failure. We may accept it as an axiom, that when an applicant for credit satisfies the standard of our requirements, we may rightfully infer that all the essential qualifications of a safe and good business-man are also possessed by him.

No effort has been made to treat this subject from the standpoint of theory or political economy. Intended, as this treatise is, for business-men and for practical use, it has been prepared as concisely as possible, and to the point —that point being, "How to make Credits." *

---

*Among business-men the term *Credits* is understood to refer to the practical functions of credit as between buyer and seller, and in this restrictive sense the word has been adopted, in contradistinction to the broader term of *Credit*.

In speaking of the credit-man throughout this book, it will be understood that all persons are meant who make sales on time, or depend on the future fulfillment of contracts.

WHOM IT CONCERNS.

This work concerns and is of paramount importance to every man engaged in trade, of whatever kind it may be, but is of special interest to the merchant and manufacturer doing necessarily a large credit business.

It concerns bookkeepers, cashiers, and accountants, upon whom devolves the duty of making credits in the absence of the regular "Credit Department," found only in the larger houses.

It concerns every young man or boy who contemplates entering mercantile life, and the information it contains will be found of great value in whatever position he may occupy. In this country every boy is a possible merchant or manufacturer, and he can not afford to neglect this branch of his business education.

It concerns every banker, for a knowledge of the elements and conditions requisite to success in his customer and debtor is of great importance. A large proportion of the loans and discounts of banks are made, not on securities actually deposited, but on the confidence felt in the borrower's methods of doing business, his standing in the community, and faith in the successful management of his undertakings. And that the Banker's confidence may not be misplaced, it is essential that he make himself a competent judge of what constitutes favorable or unfavorable conditions in the merchant or manufacturer to whom he lends his funds.

It concerns, also, lawyers, especially when acting in the capacity of attorneys for creditors. The wisdom and safety of their recommendations to their clients for further time and indulgence, in behalf of the debtor, will depend upon the attorney's knowledge of business affairs and of what constitutes safety; i. e., he should be governed in his estimate of property and assets by the same rules that govern and enable the business-man to determine questions of like character.

It concerns every man in and out of trade. Professional men, and men in all walks of life can profit by its careful perusal. It is not expected that this volume will be all-sufficient in itself, but it will at least furnish the fundamental principles, and the processes of reasoning employed in determining questions of credit.

It concerns the man out of business to-day, for to-morrow he may engage or re-engage in it; in short, as we are a nation of traders, and more credit business is done in this country than in any other, it behooves every man to know all that can be learned on this subject.

It concerns, lastly, but not least, every commercial traveler, and should be carefully read and studied by him, that he may make himself a competent judge of "Credits." A large percentage of the credits given are made on his judgment and recommendation. Some agents' opinions are entirely relied on by their respective houses, but the majority of them are not good "Credit men." Their eagerness to make a record as *salesmen* transcends all other considerations. Having been a traveling man myself at one period of my commercial life, I know from personal experience why so many fail in gaining the confidence of their firms in this capacity. An agent's recommendation for credit *should be* sufficient, and his firm should feel warranted in accepting his judgment. Where this is the case, the firm has gained a valuable co-worker, and the agent a strong foothold. To sell is one thing; to "get our pay" is of infinitely greater importance.

IMPORTANCE OF A KNOWLEDGE OF "CREDITS."

When we speak of commerce and trade, we are met by the question of their existence in a general way. There is suggested, their volume, influence of their relations on the world, and our collective welfare. Considering the subject from this standpoint, we are apt to be led to its theoretical considerations; that is, its civilizing, educational, and social influences, and to the student of political economy these offer a vast and most important field for thought and investigation. But these problems do not concern us here. We have to do with the practical affairs of life, and the question of trade being one of "bread and butter," no more serious issue could present itself.

Buying and selling constitute trade. If the transactions were all for cash, our success as merchants would simply be a question of who could buy and sell the most, and to the best advantage, and there would be no occasion for the exercise of our faculties except in buying and selling.

But what confronts us right here? It is the question of credit. As a matter of fact we do not do business for cash. We do it on credit almost wholly, and this radically changes the problem. Long and common usage, expediency, our spirit of enterprise, and our extraordinary confidence in each other, have established the custom of parting with our property on promises of future payment, and after once parting with it, we hold as a substitute, written or verbal, the buyer's promise to pay, and that is all. The discharge of this promise rests on the buyer's honesty, ability, experience, and a multitude of other factors. If the buyer is honest, our safety depends, mainly, on his success, and this, again, is dependent on his qualifications and circumstances over which he may or may not be able to exercise control.

The practical and all-important questions then are, to make sure of our payment when due, and that the men we sell to are both willing and able to do as they agree. The ability to sell the most goods and do the largest business, does not in itself determine a man's success; in fact, observation proves that this is often done unwisely and against his best interests.

Commerce and credit are inseparable. They are not only inseparable, but a judicious exercise of credit-giving is the more important of the two. Before delivering our goods to another's custody, our first concern must be the reliability of the custodian or buyer, and the probability of getting our money, and with it our profit, which is the sole object of doing business. This being decided, pro or con, we then make or do not make the sale. This proves our position—that our ability as judges, when to sell and when not, comes first in importance, and that of salesmen comes second.

Practically, credit is incidental to trade, and in our daily transactions the major part of trade is done on credit; i. e., it is dependent on our confidence in the buyer; but *blind* confidence is not meant, nor will it answer. Our faith in men must result from the exercise of good judgment, large experience, a knowledge of men and things, and their fitness to each other. Is our confidence justifiable in any given case? That is the question. That it very often is not, we have learned to our sorrow.

As above stated, in no country is credit so generally and so lavishly given as in this. Our whole commercial fabric rests on it. Every individual welfare, to a greater or less extent, depends on credit, and the wise use of it. As a problem of such consequence and as a prime factor in our individual success, can the importance of its study, and our thorough mastery of it, be over-estimated? No; but that it has not received the attention it deserves is a fact painfully regretted by thousands.

Hon. Edward Everett, in an address delivered before the Mercantile Library Association in Boston in 1838, stated his conviction as follows: "I should deem the formation of sound and sober views on the study of credit one of the most desirable portions of a young merchant's education." The practical merchant is even more impressed with the importance of the subject, as a result of his daily experience.

Much as it is desired by the author that this treatise might lead his readers to infallibility in making credits, that is a thing beyond his expectations. But this much is certain, in calling your attention to the subject, and a comprehensive study of it, not alone by these pages, but drawing on your own resources of experience and observation, it is impossible that you will be other than largely benefited; and if nothing more be accomplished than to interest you in the study, I shall be amply repaid. The benefit to you, in that case, will be analogous to that of a man face to face with a great danger, of which he has been forewarned and for which he is thoroughly prepared.

That the most rigid adherence to the rules here laid down will avoid loss in every instance, is not expected. The best of business-men, the most conservative and experienced, "miss it" quite often enough. But there is a wide margin between the maximum of losses usually sustained and the minimum to which they may be reduced, a difference sufficient in itself to make one man happy and prosperous, and another wretched and bankrupt.

In addition to the chief object before us, which

is to become competent judges of whom it is safe to trust, the suggestions offered will also be valuable in regulating our own conduct, so that we may share the confidence of others, and be entitled to credit ourselves.

LOSSES BY FAILURE.

BUSINESS FAILURES, 1877 TO 1886, INCLUSIVE.

YEAR.	NUMBER IN BUSINESS.	NUMBER FAILURES.	LIABILITIES.	AVERAGE LIABILITIES.	PROPORTION FAILURES.
1877	652,006	8,872	$190,669,936	21,491	1 in 73
1878	674,741	10,478	234,383,132	22,369	1 " 64
1879	702,157	6,658	98,149,053	14,741	1 " 105
1880	746,823	4,735	65,752,000	13,886	1 " 158
1881	781,689	5,582	81,155,932	14,538	1 " 140
1882	822,256	6,738	101,547,564	15,062	1 " 122
1883	863,993	9,184	172,874,172	18,823	1 " 94
1884	904,759	10,968	226,343,427	20,636	1 " 82
1885	919,990	10,637	124,220,321	11,679	1 " 86
1886	969,841	9,834	114,644,119	11,703	1 " 98
	8,038,255	83,686	1,409,739,656	164,928	10.22

These figures, like many other statistics, convey very little meaning taken by themselves. They have no particular significance, except, perhaps, that they look large to the casual reader. Whether in fact, and in face of the transactions they represent, they are large or small, no adequate idea is furnished. Only by a comparison with the business of previous years are we enabled to judge of the present status and determine whether it is more prosperous, or otherwise, to those engaged in it. But for the close student, and for the man who undertakes to deduce exact facts and figures, it is necessary that he have some basis to work upon; yet statistics furnishing such data are almost entirely wanting and are not supplied by our statistical bureau. Nor would the labor required to ascertain such figures as are needed be warranted by any private individual, or even trade journals. Nothing short of a "Bureau of Commercial Statistics," under the direct patronage of the commercial industries themselves, will accomplish anything in this direction with the necessary degree of exactitude. Such a bureau, in charge of a competent business-man of large experience, one who knows what kind of information to collect and select, would be of incalculable benefit in various ways. The information and figures attainable at present of the manufacturing and mercantile interests, particularly the latter, are very vague and meager, and neither assimilation nor approximation is easy or possible.

For instance, to ascertain the percentage of losses sustained by our merchants, it would be necessary to know the total mercantile transactions of the country, the capital invested in mercantile pursuits, and the losses by failures of this class. These data would enable us to arrive at the per cent. of loss, both on the capital and the volume of business.

The table given above comprises a period of ten years, and the condition of the country during that time—from 1877 to 1886—fluctuated from extraordinary depression to great activity and prosperity, and back again, thus giving us a fair general average. The number of firms that failed each year during the ten years is one

LOSSES BY FAILURE.

in ninety; the failures aggregate the grand total of $1,409,739,656, equal to nearly one-half of the total (approximated) capital invested in both mercantile and manufacturing business, as shown further on. The yearly average of losses amount to $140,000,000, in round numbers. Of course, the entire liabilities of the failed concerns which these figures represent were not lost. We may assume that 30 per cent. was recovered; but this was temporarily tied up, and practically the whole sum was unavailable, so far as the effect and injury to the creditor class was concerned. Deducting from the ten years' average of $140,000,000, 30 per cent. as having been realized, the *net annual* loss sustained by merchants and manufacturers is nearly $100,000,000.

From the best estimates obtainable, the capital invested in mercantile and manufacturing enterprises in the United States, in 1880, amounted to about four thousand million dollars. One quarter of this may be supposed to have been removed from the danger line of the credit system. As nearly as possible, we want to arrive at the capital that is affected by and dependent on this system, and we have, approximately, three thousand millions of capital thus employed. One hundred millions annual loss on this sum is equal to $3\frac{1}{3}$ per cent. on the total capital.

To form an estimate of the percentage of loss

on the sales or transactions of the country, we may multiply the capital by four, as we turn it over probably that number of times, at least. That gives us a volume of business equal to twelve thousand millions (twelve billions), subject to the vicissitudes of the credit system. One hundred millions losses makes eighty-three-one-hundreths of one per cent. (.83-100) loss on this volume of business.

The approximate correctness of these percentages is verified by taking a certain number of business houses and computing the average of their losses on a basis of capital invested. Most of them do not calculate their losses on the basis of capital employed, but on that of the volume of business transacted; but here, also, we find the estimate verified by actual figures, taken and averaged from a large number of individual cases. Proportionately, the larger houses lose less than the smaller ones; the percentage decreases with the increase in the volume of business, and the reasons are obvious.

I desire now to call attention to the question: Do mercantile pursuits render the losses usually sustained imperative and unavoidable? In a measure, yes; but in a larger measure, no. They are chiefly the result of carelessness, inexperience, and a deficiency of proper discipline on the part of our business-men. It is a lack of knowledge and judgment in the matter of giving credit; or, if not these, it is carelessness or recklessness.

The importance of this factor in individual success can not be overestimated, and to illustrate it we have only to take the average business house for the last twenty years, and figure up the losses sustained by it, and compare the sum total, with compound interest, with its present financial status, and we shall find that it has lost more than the capital accumulated during the period.

This may seem a very broad assertion, but figures have been obtained from a sufficient number of houses to warrant the conclusion. Nor were these houses selected especially for their extra good or bad management; they represent what is wanted for our purpose, namely, a fair average.

From the foregoing facts and figures, it is apparent that we are doing a large amount of business, not alone for nothing, but at a loss of capital, for the goods we sell are part of our capital, and, if lost, that much capital is lost. It may be asserted that the merchant adds the probable percentage of his losses to the selling price of his goods, or, in other words, figures his profit by that much more. In that case the merchant would not be the loser, for the solvent buyers would make good the loss. But this view can not be accepted at the present day. To meet competition and hold and extend his trade, the merchant is forced to fix his profit without any allowance for losses. Whatever loss is sustained by reason of bad debts, is to that extent a drain upon his earnings and resources. It follows, then, since competition enforces nearly uniform profits upon all in the same line of trade, that the concern losing the least, comes nearest realizing its calculations.

MERCANTILE REPORTS.

The mercantile report is one of the many innovations of modern business life, and is as much a necessity to-day as any one of the other helpful needs and agents enjoyed by this, over past generations. Though far from perfect—in fact, quite imperfect—it is, nevertheless, an indispensable adjunct to our present methods. It affords facilities to the business community without which our extensive relations would be materially curtailed, and credits, and therefore business generally, suffer serious restrictions. That the mercantile report fills an absolute want is furthermore evidenced by the very general patronage of the mercantile agencies by business-men. In addition to quarterly and semi-annually revised reference books, they also undertake to furnish their subscribers detailed reports of facts and figures concerning the financial status of every dealer in the country. How far they succeed in giving reliable data is left for the patrons of these institutions to determine. They certainly succeed sufficiently to create an ever-increasing demand for their labors. The steady improvement year after year of the agency service is a noteworthy and encouraging feature.

In the nature of things, infallibility is something the mercantile agency can never hope to attain, since stability of capital actually employed at any given time and in any given business, can not be depended upon. Men do not always confine themselves to their regular vocations, and capital is thus often diverted from its legitimate operations and devoted to speculative purposes, which may or may not be profitable. The American business community is especially prone to speculation, and, as speculation goes, it is largely at the expense of the regular business. Nor have we any remedy against this, not even when the creditor's capital is directly used and jeopardized for the purpose. No restrictions are possible to regulate the exercise of individual judgment in regard to the employment of money once in possession, either in fee simple or in trust. Whether success or failure attends a particular venture, are matters of which the outside world is left in ignorance, especially if failure should result. If successful, no one finds fault; if otherwise, it is too late to avail.

From this alone it will be seen that the financial status of business concerns would vary considerably, even from one month to another. Ratings would require more frequent revision than is possible with the present facilities of the agencies in order to cover these changes of conditions. It is usually only subsequent developments that bring these matters to light, and that at a time when the knowledge of the facts ceases to be of any benefit to us.

But diversion of capital from its legitimate uses, and to purposes not at all speculative, is also a matter of importance. Many businessmen, from miscalculation and poor judgment, invest too large a portion of their working capital in permanent improvements and outside ventures, not necessarily of a speculative nature, and thereby tie up capital which should have remained a working force. Although real estate and permanent improvements should constitute the best representatives of capital invested, and indicate the highest order of assets, yet we know from experience that this class of property is not convertible at will in the event of failure, nor is it, as a rule, available to the creditors. The mercantile agency, however, has no right to ignore capital thus invested; it is obliged to give it a place among the assets and make its ratings accordingly. For this reason "the keys" used by the various agencies to denote capital are less to be relied upon than the report itself, for the latter gives details and shows what the capital consists of and is used in, and from these we can make our own deductions. The nature of the assets has much to do with the value of the ratings for the purpose of basing credits.

This much is certain, if we could always make sure of getting reliable reports, whatever their source might be, the credit man's task would be made easier, and losses by bad debts would be reduced to a minimum. The weak feature of the mercantile agency system is its dependence on correspondents, who are expected to give their time and services gratuitously, or nearly so, and we necessarily have to contend with frequent negligence, inaccuracy, and incompetency, and sometimes even personal favoritism or prejudice, as the case may be. That this has been and is being remedied to a considerable extent by the better class of agencies, we have evidence from the improving quality of service rendered. Good services command good pay, and it is due the business world that the agencies secure competent correspondents and pay and charge accordingly. We can afford to pay well for reliable reports; unreliable ones are dear at any price.

Quite a prominent feature of many of the collection agencies is their list of attorneys throughout the country, who are under contract (without pay however) to report the standing of business-men in their respective localities. As auxiliaries, and used to corroborate other statements, they possess merit, and are made use of to a considerable extent. But the attorneys perform their labors entirely gratis, and the reports from this source seldom furnish details, but simply offer opinions that parties are supposed to be good or otherwise—generally good. The attorneys expect to establish a large clientage through the acquaintance made in this way, and their compensation, as reporters, is expected to come from professional services in the future.

On the whole, excepting, of course, many inaccuracies and misconceptions of facts, the mercantile agency report can be said to lean toward unbiased and truthful statements of ascertainable facts. Human nature inclines to well-meaning statements concerning our fellowmen, and this being so, we may be tolerably certain that a derogatory report has something in it for a foundation, and the credit-man should be slow to ignore its unfavorable comments.

ANALYSIS OF STATEMENTS OR REPORTS.

In the preceding chapter, mercantile agency reports only were discussed, but it was not intended to be inferred that business houses were dependent on these for information exclusively. Information regarding the standing of people in trade is obtained from various sources, and not infrequently directly from the applicants for credit. The object of getting a report is, of course, to gain such information as will enable us to determine whether a certain dealer is entitled to credit or not, and if so, to what extent. But what class of information do we require to determine this question, and that will enable us to arrive at an intelligent conclusion?

The farmer who contemplates buying lands and settling in a new territory, will want to know many things before he invests his money and locates. His experience and knowledge of his vocation have taught him that simply buying so many acres of land, regardless of internal or external conditions, would be very unwise; therefore, before he invests, he learns about the soil, its condition and adaptation, the climate, the markets, the facilities for transporting his produce, and a great many other things. A farmer should know just what is necessary for him to investigate in order to make a wise selection; and a practical farmer does know. With a business-man, in making credits, it is precisely the same. There are certain things concerning a would-be debtor, of which he must inform himself in order to judge understandingly.

As in the farmer's case, our experience and business education have taught us that our safety as creditors is dependent on many contingencies; on qualities of mind and heart of the debtor; on his mental, moral, and financial status, and also on his surrounding relationships, etc.

Now we find, by applying the rules of analysis to business, that it is resolvable into certain constituent elements, and that its success, and our safety as creditors, is dependent upon the existence and proper combination of these elements. One of the elements or requisites is honesty; another, ability; another, capital, and so on; and when we have completed our analysis, we find that we have thirty different and distinct elements to which we should have answers, and on which it is important to get information. Each one of these elements constitutes an important factor, although some are of more consequence than others. To take one spoke out of a wheel would weaken it, though not perceptibly, perhaps. Industry and capital in business may be likened to the hub; ability, experience, and honesty to the fellies and tire. The spokes come in to combine the two into a symmetrical and effective whole. In like manner the thirty elements or requisites go to make up a whole, by showing us the constituent parts necessary to insure our safety as creditors, and success as business-men.

Each one of the following elements is susceptible of individual analysis, to which the first part of this book is devoted. We take them without reference to their relative importance. The first thing we are usually made cognizant of is the nature of the business in which the applicant is engaged, the next thing is invariably the place where he is located. We therefore commence with:

No. 1. Nature of the Business.
No. 2. Locality.
No. 3. Character and Habits.
No. 4. Ability.
No. 5. Experience.
No. 6. Application and Industry.
No. 7. Business Education.
No. 8. Honesty.
No. 9. Economy.
No. 10. Married or Single.
No. 11. Age.
No. 12. Capital.
No. 13. Assets—Stock and Personal Property.

ANALYSIS OF STATEMENTS OR REPORTS. 37

No. 14. Assets—Accounts and Bills Receivable.
No. 15. Assets—Real Estate—Exemptions.
No. 16. Liabilities.
No. 17. Volume of Business.
No. 18. Antecedents.
No. 19. Competition.
No. 20. Punctuality.
No. 21. Productive or Non-productive.
No. 22. Doing Business as Agents.
No. 23. Partnerships.
No. 24. Doubtful Credits.
No. 25. Joint Stock Companies and Coöperative Associations.
No. 26. Women in Trade.
No. 27. Chattel Mortgages and Other Liens.
No. 28. Insurance.
No. 29. Miscellaneous Information.
No. 30. Old Customers.

It might seem that to embody all these questions in a statement, or rather to exact information on them all, would make a very lengthy report, and be asking too much labor from the agency or correspondent. But this is not so. An ordinary report, such as we all receive in our daily business transactions, is here submitted, which will be found to give satisfactory answers to every one of the series of questions. The numbers in the report have reference to the corresponding numbers in the foregoing series of questions—like numbers representing questions and answers.

J. M. S.—(1) Hardware and stoves. (2) Chicago, Ill. (19) In business here since 1876. (11) Age fifty. (10) Man of family. (21) Tinner by trade. (9) Saved up $300, which was his capital when starting. (18) Came from Ohio. (3) Character and habits good. (8) Reputed honest and upright in his dealings. (4 and 7) Fair education and business ability. (6) Attentive and industrious. (9) Economical. (13) Last inventory, stock $10,000. (14) Accounts due him, $5,000. (15) Homestead, $3,000. (13) Other personal property, $1,500. Total assets, $19,500. (16) Liabilities: Owing for stock on open accounts, $4,500. No other indebtedness. (12) Net surplus, $15,000. (12) Net capital in business, $12,000. (28) Insurance on stock, $8,000. (20) Prompt in meeting his engagements. (17) Sales last year, $35,000.

ANYALSIS AND REMARKS.

This report answers every one of our questions, though some of them only inferentially. It says nothing directly of his experience, but we infer that he has had that for the last thirteen years. As to partnership, he is perhaps wise in not having any, and the question does not pertain to him; he is alone, the report says. His antecedents, back of thirteen years ago, do not interest us; his record while here is sufficient. The report says: "No indebtedness except on open account," so there are no chattel mortgages or liens. In regard to doing business as agent, women in trade, stock companies, the report answers all these questions inferentially.

We may say in regard to this man that he is good for his business requirements and entitled to credit up to the full limit, which, being a prudent man, as we see, he will never ask.

He has succeeded in building up a lucrative business, and in accumulating a moderate capital, which is all of an available character. To do this he must have combined application with intelligent management and economy. His available assets are $16,500. He owes $4,500, but would be safe for an indebtedness of $10,000, or even $12,000. His accounts due him are in good proportion to the business done, and show that he has only about sixty days' sales outstanding, from which we infer that he looks after his collections closely. The accounts are, therefore, not of long standing, and presumably are collectible. His methods of doing business do not indicate that he would include in his showing, old, worthless bills. His annual sales indicate prudence and conservatism. Many firms with less capital would undertake to do more business.

This case is not difficult to decide; in fact, it is an exceptionally easy one. The above indicates the usual *modus operandi* of examining a report, and the line of reasoning employed to arrive at a decision.

For the purpose of furnishing material for analysis, and to enable those of my readers to whom the facilities are not offered, and who seek, possibly, preparatory knowledge in the "science of credits," I have selected a number of mercantile agency reports which will be found on pages 174 to 199. These are all actual reports received in the course of business; only such changes being made as are necessary to avoid identification.

The following thirty chapters will take up the analytical series in the order enumerated.

NATURE OF THE BUSINESS.

When we contemplate investing in business, the first point of consideration with us is to determine the degree of risk that pertains to it. In a large sense the interests of the creditor and the investor are identical. One risks his capital and time; the other his merchandise, and the question is, therefore, of equal importance to both. Now, we know that some lines of business are more hazardous than others, and this question of necessity constitutes an important factor for us to consider. In the analysis of our report we were called upon to investigate a retail hardware business in its relation to reliability and risk. Of this we know, from past and present observation, that it is both safe and legitimate, and that, with fair attention and ability, it will always do well by its proprietor. It has comparatively few drawbacks, and is exempt from many of the ills to which other lines of business are subject. Losses by reason of old stock or styles, by damage to goods, by age, temperature, or otherwise, are only the result of gross negligence and inattention in this business, and herein it has quite an advantage over others in which, from various causes, more or less shrinkage is unavoidable. So far, then, as the nature of the business under consideration is concerned, we call it exceptionally safe in fairly capable hands, and can dismiss the question, so far as it relates to this report. But this is only one of many.

Different lines of business are subject to different ills, and more of them, which affect both the debtor and creditor. It is, therefore, incumbent on us to know the detrimental or hazardous features in each case. A stock of seasonable goods always has more risk attached than one of staple goods, that moves every day, and we find correspondingly more failures. The most hazardous goods for the retail hardware dealer, for instance, are stoves and heating apparatus, and many a good businessman has been bankrupted by an overstock of these, brought about by an untoward season or some other cause that prevented sale in the short time such goods are usually in demand.

Of staple lines of business, a grocer's stock is probably the easiest to convert; but the grocer makes more bad accounts than the hardware man, where the ordinary credit system is rulable. In addition to losses from this source, the city retail grocer has another serious drawback to success, and that is the great expense attending his business, which seems unavoidable if he desires to retain and advance his position in the trade. It results in this, that the closest management becomes necessary to success, and the money-making city retail grocers are few compared with the number engaged in that business.

But it is not necessary to enter into details of every line of business, and to discuss the advantages and disadvantages of each.

Every line of business has established for itself its own terms, either long or short time, or cash, and these have come to be recognized by the trade at large, and are enforced as if they were law. Now, we find that the most necessary articles to the community, such as flour, meats, sugar, etc., are sold nearest to a cash basis—in fact, they are sold for cash only from first hands. We here establish a starting point, and as articles of commerce become less necessary to existence and comfort, we find the terms lengthened out in proportion. This law will be found to hold good throughout. From time to time, as profits on certain lines of goods are cut down, the time is shortened also, and this, too, is in conformity with the laws of commerce. The greater the profit, the greater the risk that can be taken, and the longer the time that can be, and is, given.

Seasonable goods are sold on long time to facilitate their distribution, but they are made payable when the season for their use comes, and they are then sold for cash or on time, according to their nature.

The trade in certain lines adopt certain terms, and their uniform adoption exacts their acceptance by the community at large. It is not necessary to state here the maxim, that the shorter the credit the less the risk, and vice versa. That is self-evident. A business in which the transactions are for cash, attracts to itself moneyed men only, who are prepared to meet its demands on them, and there is little or no risk in the ordinary sense. On the other hand, when time is given, it opens the gates to speculation on the future, and taking chances on what should, and under favorable circumstances would, transpire. Therefore, the longer the time, the greater will be the opportunity for speculative indulgence, and the greater the risk to the creditor.

LOCALITY.

In the case of the mercantile report cited on page 38 we have to do with a large city, the metropolis of a large section of country, with its vast and diversified interests. All the different industries of the surrounding country, in a measure of the whole country, are tributary to it as a commercial center. Its own immense population, and the varied enterprises and industries within its own limits, create demand and supply for an inconceivable variety and quantity of wares and work. The business of a large city, therefore, is not dependent upon any one particular industry, whether within itself or tributary to it. The prosperity of all the industries in and out of it, would mean exceptionally good times for the city dealers, and a depression in one or more would only measurably affect it.

With city dealers and business houses we have always to consider that the competition for trade is very great, and the expense of doing business equally so. It is always an open question, therefore, whether a new concern can get on a paying basis or not. If it can secure a share of the business from the start, it is well. If not, a long struggle for existence ensues, which time alone determines, and meanwhile the status of the debtor is a doubtful one. A city merchant, with an established business, has fewer risks and interruptions to contend with, than where one industry is depended on for the support of the community where he is located.

We are called upon now to speak of some of the leading industries that control the welfare of different localities. We have farming, mining, lumbering, manufacturing, and other centers. Locality is an important factor in determining credits, since it gives us somewhat of an idea of the risk incurred.

In old farming communities, credit can be given with a liberal hand, and it depends mostly on the honesty and ability of the debtor as to meeting his obligations. Crops may be poor some years, and prices low, and some indulgences may be needed, but otherwise there are no contingencies likely to arise of an unfavorable character. This class of trade is not, perhaps, the most profitable to the retailer, but it is the safest.

In lumber regions, the people as a class have plenty of money in certain seasons and none in others, and the result is that the merchants there, as a rule, have to carry and be carried. Their customers are largely composed of employés who are paid at the close of the season's work, and meantime they have to be trusted for the necessaries and comforts of life. As long as lumbering can be done profitably the merchants are safe, but "hard times" in that industry means dire calamity to everybody interested, whether directly or indirectly.

Mining regions offer rich rewards to dealers while "the boom is on," and while they are in active operation. High wages are paid usually, and people spend liberally, for both necessaries and luxuries. But we have seen enough of mining towns and localities to know what vicissitudes they are subject to. What was a thriving town three years ago is a deserted camp to-day. New mining towns can never be depended on to "stay put," and even the older mines are frequently closed for one cause or another and the income of the population is stopped for a time. All these interruptions affect those who supply goods, both wholesale and retail. The shrewd merchant does not necessarily avoid these districts. The trade is large and profitable while it lasts. He secures a share of it, but retires before the collapse, for there are usually sufficient warnings given to those who are on the alert for signs.

In exclusively manufacturing centers and localities, where the dealers depend almost wholly on the employés of the factories for patronage, the conditions are *not* such as to strengthen the stability or reliability of the dealers. They depend, not alone on the employés for their trade, but generally carry them from one pay-day to another. In case of a shut-down, the dealer is not only liable to be left without customers, but he has also a number of bills of very doubtful character for the time being, at least until other work can be obtained or the mills start up again. Those who have been in business during the last ten years in such localities, especially when strikes and lock-outs have occurred, can appreciate the situation.

There will always be traders wherever there is a demand for goods, no matter what the conditions or risks may be. That locality constitutes an important factor, and that our security and the promptness of our customers is better or worse accordingly, needs no further discussion. The credit-man should not fail to consider that the status which would be satisfactory of a dealer in one place would not necessarily be so in another.

Another point that deserves mention here is the accessibility of your customers. You want them, preferably, where they can be reached by the ordinary methods used for collecting. A large percentage of our collections are made by drafts sent to banks. Towns that have no banks, and are too small even to support a lawyer, place the creditor at great disadvantage when he undertakes to collect.

To insure collections in these remote places, it is necessary to send claims to attorneys often residing at a distance, and this makes the expense quite onerous. Many people will pay a draft drawn through a bank when they would be very dilatory in remitting.

Another point also presents itself, viz.: the relation of locality to distance from the markets. A retailer in Chicago, for instance, can do a large business on a comparatively small capital. He is not required to carry stock beyond his daily or weekly wants. He can buy and sell, from "hand to mouth," and draw his supplies from the jobber, who practically answers the purpose of a warehouse.

On the other hand, the dealer who is remotely situated from the markets is obliged to carry stock enough to last from one to six months, according to distance and location. The city dealer can carry a full assortment in small quantities with one thousand dollars, we will say, while in the other case the same assortment, with the increased quantities necessary, will involve a very much larger capital. It is apparent, therefore, that to do a certain volume of business, more capital is required in one locality than in another.

LOCALITY—CONTINUED.

COLLECTION LAWS.

In some States the debtor has more protection than in others, and this is a vital point to be considered in making credits. The difference in the protection granted to debtors in different localities, does not go so far as to make a debtor pay when he has nothing to pay with. Devoutly as such a law might be desired in the interest of commerce, its fruition will continue a thing to be hoped for, but never to be realized. But the point I wish to make is this: In some States, notably in the older and more populous ones, an action can be commenced, judgment obtained, and execution levied in ten days, in amounts under $200, and in twenty to forty days a judgment is usually obtainable for any amount, and if property can be found it can be satisfied forthwith. But in the Western and Southern States the law's delays, from one cause and another, operate most disastrously to the creditor class. The sessions of the courts are farther apart, and it takes longer to try cases and bring them to a focus. After a decision is finally reached, the debtor's protection comes in under the head of exemptions, stays, etc.

The laws in the newer States seem to operate with especial reference to the protection of the

LOCALITY—CONTINUED.

inhabitants, both purposely and incidentally; nor may we question their justness or expediency. New countries must offer protection in proportion to the hardships that await new comers and the risks they have to take. It is simply the credit-man's duty to know what the laws are, and a synopsis of these is easily obtained.

In the Territories, for instance, we find that a man of moderate circumstances may claim as exempt, nearly all he possesses. He is entitled to personal and miscellaneous property to the extent of $1,500, to be selected by the debtor, which may mean twice the amount in fact. He is entitled to a homestead not exceeding 160 acres of land, or one acre in town, without limitation of value of buildings and improvements thereon.

It will be seen, then, that with the generality of dealers, in those localities, the creditor has no legal foothold, and it is important to be cognizant of this fact when we extend credit to them.

In general, and when the buyer is possessed of the average capital, of from $1,000 to $5,000, we are not justified in basing credit on his capital. Our safety lies in his honor, and it is not prudent to rely on anything else. The applicant for credit should, therefore, have a well-established reputation for upright and honorable dealings in those localities.

CHARACTER AND HABITS.

The most important items on which we need information are the character and habits of the applicant for credit, and if these are not good we have not much use for him in any capacity, especially that of debtor. Ability, experience, and even capital would hardly compensate for the lack of these two concomitant elements in the make-up of a debtor, any more than in the case of an agent or trusted employé.

Character and habits are here treated together, for the reason that they are practically inseparable—for our purpose at least. A man may have exceptionally good habits and lack good character withal—in fact, be a thorough-bred scoundrel. On the other hand, he may have proven himself a first class, upright businessman, of the highest integrity, worthy of confidence, and yet have some very bad habits. From a business point of view, and where a reputation for honesty and honorable dealings has been established, we may be justified in looking lightly on some personal short-comings in the matter of habits. But this view of the case could only find justification where a would-be debtor had been established in trade for a long period. On general principles, however, one could not afford to ignore a man's habits where a credit or a trust was involved.

Old established houses have their record. The great difficulty is in determining the character of men just starting in business. Such may, and probably have, served an apprenticeship as clerks, but nothing can really be known of their character as principals and business managers until time and opportunity are given to develop them. A man's habits, on the other hand, we can know, as they would be much the same either as employé or as principal.

In extending credit, the character and habits of the party asking it should be searchingly inquired into and all the facts ascertained. Our security as creditors depends on these factors more largely than on any other two. No applicant for credit is entitled to it unless his record for both honesty and sobriety is above reproach. The men of moderate ability, and of good character and habits, are the "standbys" in trade, but reversing this order, we are liable to reverse our fortunes if we make them our debtors.

Because the exceptions prove the rule, we can lay it down as a rule, that business-men who are addicted to habitual and excessive drinking, etc., are undesirable debtors; not altogether for the reason that they drink, but because of the inevitable consequences entailed through it; namely, neglect of business, loss of time, and unwarranted expense.

It is supposable that no sales are ever made without expectations of payment, and yet we find that men of all shades of character, and even "shady characters," constantly figure in the reported failures of the country. That somebody has taken stock in them is self-evident. If they did not owe anybody they would have no need or inducement to fail. The fact that they do owe is *prima facie* evidence that their credit was good in some quarter, at least. The assumption can hardly hold good that the creditors of dubious characters in trade were cognizant of the fact of such dubiousness when selling to them. We must, therefore, charge this indiscriminate and lavish dispensation of credit, not to a knowledge of the facts, but to negligence in obtaining them. And this is where the weakness of most creditors lies. The time to inquire into character and habits, and other things necessary to be known, is when you make the credit, and if there is any doubt, take the benefit of the doubt yourself.

ABILITY.

Ability in the abstract is one thing; ability in the line of our special vocation is quite another. No matter how great a man's ability, he can not hope to master every calling. To select the vocation suited to our special ability, is the most important step in a man's career. It surpasses all others in its influence on our future destiny. If phrenology could be reduced to the scientific accuracy which is claimed for it, it would be a most valuable aid in determining our special aptitude for this or that occupation, and failures would be the exception instead of the rule.

Taking cognizance of the fact, as our statisticians show, that only five per cent. of our business-men succeed, we are forced to the conclusion that something is radically wrong. It certainly is not lack of business that is or can be done, but lack of ability as merchants that is the cause of so many failures, and here is the root of half the evils incident to mercantile life. Though a man be possessed of good ability, if his efforts are misdirected and not in the line of his particular talents, his endeavors will necessarily come short of his real capacity.

Mercantile life can be and is entered by people without any preparatory schooling, and without reference to fitness. Any man with a few dollars and a desire for something to do can become a merchant, and he naturally turns his attention to it as offering the greatest inducements with the least requirements. How, then, can we expect that mercantile pursuits should succeed, as a rule, when they are largely in the hands of incompetent men? The law of the survival of the fittest dooms them to failure.

The most eminent lawyers and world-renowned doctors would not necessarily make good merchants or manufacturers, and vice versa. It may be presumed that the fact of their greatness in their respective professions lies in having chosen vocations suited to their particular ability. The same may be said, and with equal truth, of successful merchants.

To undertake to analyze and define ability, and the particular ability required to be a good merchant, is too large a subject to be handled here, and belongs more to the "Science of Business" than to the "Science of Credits." But we will state some of the qualities and experience that observation has taught us go to make up the successful merchant.

The sum total of the qualities that make a successful career possible may be defined as constituting business ability. Trifling as some of these qualities may seem in themselves, they are of the utmost importance in forming the combination.

First, the merchant must be a good judge of

human nature and of character. At every turn this quality will be required, and is especially important in the selection of co-workers and assistants. Great achievements and the building up of large enterprises are not possible without good assistants, and the quality of these depends on him who selects them. Men have been known to succeed in an eminent degree with hardly any other qualification, that was discernable at least, than that of being able to surround themselves with good men, either partners or otherwise. This, of course, is not a trait that can be cultivated very much. It is natural to some, the same as other special gifts, but it is of the utmost importance to all business-men.

The merchant must be a good judge of values. This is essential, as profitable sales depend on judicious purchases. The trader is born with an intuitive knowledge of values and goods, of the needs and desires of the people, and that knowledge is his stock in trade to commence with. He has also a quick insight into the relations between actual needs and "man's progressive wants," and measure of pecuniary ability to gratify the same.

The merchant must have large executive ability, and be an organizer. New combinations are constantly forming as his business expands and conditions change, and he must be equal to the emergency of meeting them and adapting himself to them. Quick discrimination and ready decision are indispensable factors in his make-up.

He must have the quality within him to desire to keep and to accumulate. All men have this desire to keep, in theory, but not in practice. To practice it, requires self-denial, and that is by no means a universal trait of character.

The merchant's business is one of endless detail, and the closest attention is requisite. It is not the large affairs only that require supervision; unless the small matters are looked after, large ones will never present themselves.

Singleness of purpose in the merchant is essential to success, coupled, as it must be, with indefatigable energy. A man's energies must be bent in one direction and to one purpose for the achievement of success in his particular line. No man has more temptations offered him for outside ventures and money-making schemes than the merchant, and it requires a strong make-up to be proof against them. The cause of innumerable financial wrecks can be found here.

To be a good financier is an important requisite in the merchant; but not in the sense in which that term is generally used. The term financier is presented to us in the light of a man who goes head-over-heels in debt and complications, and then extricates himself as best he may. The good merchant avoids complications that might imperil control and thorough mastery over his own affairs; his obligations are based on certainties to fulfill, so far, at least, as human sagacity can determine.

These are some of the elemental traits that go to make up a good merchant. Others could be added, but for the purpose of this chapter further analysis is unnecessary.

EXPERIENCE.

Of ability, experience, education, character, and habits, it would be difficult to say which is the least important or most indispensable. Each would seem to be a *sine qua non*, though incomplete in itself. To engage in any business without experience nowadays, a man might be likened to a ship without a rudder, and the chances for the inexperienced are growing less and less each year, in the ratio that our standard of knowledge and experience is raised. In the country we often find good farmers allured to store-keeping. They can illy be spared as farmers, as they are trained and experienced in that calling, but as merchants they could well be spared, and usually are, after a short probation, when they find themselves wiser, but poorer, men. The credit-man calculates on about how long the "farm money" will hold out, and extends his accommodations accordingly.

The aggregate knowledge that has been acquired by personal observation and actual trials is called experience. The kind of experience we are looking for is of a specific character and confined to some one branch of business, and there is no department in trade to-day that does not offer sufficient scope to monopolize all a man's time and attention.

The more difficult any business or profession is to learn, the fewer will be the competitors to invade it, and herein lies our compensation for its mastery.

Every business has its ups and downs, its good and bad sides. Experience in a particular business enables us to foresee and provide against emergencies, which the inexperienced mind is incapable of doing; and, further, it enables us, in a large degree, to control circumstances, instead of being controlled by them. We select our doctors and lawyers from the ranks of those who can give us the benefits of a long practice and consequent experience.

The experienced man is always equal to the emergencies as they arise in his special department. He has been through all phases of "dilemmas," and they neither dishearten nor demoralize him. His experience has furnished him with the resources to combat or ward off the impending danger. He knows how to avoid the shallows and the rocks, because he has learned exactly where they are. What would appear to others insurmountable barriers, cause him no uneasiness. He has learned to distinguish the path that leads by easy stages.

Men going into new lines of business are constantly at sea, and the elements seem always contending against their struggling craft. The man brought up to a particular business, however, feels as safe and secure in it as if it were a fortress, and is able to withstand any ordinary assaults from without with comparative composure. This much for experience.

On the other hand, take a man without experience, and every mole-hill appears like a mountain, and as one is surmounted another looms up before him. "Hills peep o'er hills, and Alps on Alps arise." We are largely creatures of habit. The experience acquired by the father is, in a large part, the inheritance of the son. Members of successive generations follow in each other's footsteps in their selection of occupations, and the experience and accumulated stock of knowledge of one generation is readily appropriated by the next. The average boy, brought up in his father's store, is conversant with nearly every detail of the business, and seems to come by it without any particular effort.

Capital and experience yoked together make a strong combination and lend to our business ventures the greatest probability of success. Experience alone is capable of acquiring capital, and of commanding it. Confidence in the individual to manage wisely, and with experience, is the key to credit, and in procuring credit we procure capital to use in the furtherance of our special enterprises. But the possessor of capital alone, without experience, is dependent on others who have experience to make his monetary possessions productive, and this accounts for the large amount of money that is always at the command of *experienced* men. Experience, therefore, in being able to command capital, is a most important factor. Millions of dollars are intrusted to the managers of large corporations, men whose experience is considered a sufficient guarantee to the investors that their funds will be safely and profitably invested, and we see in this the force of our argument. To experience, therefore, quite as much as to capital, do we owe the advancement of our commercial and industrial interests. The surplus accumulations of capital, not less than the capital owned and controlled by inexperienced individuals, is thus brought into productive use.

To acquire experience requires time and patient toil. Money can combine with it advantageously, but it can not buy it, though the instances are not rare where one is exchanged for the other. Money is very often exchanged for experience, though under protest on the part of the money-owner.

In making a credit we need hardly call attention to the importance of considering the applicant's experience.

APPLICATION AND INDUSTRY.

John Jay said of a contemporary: "Had his application been equal to his talents, his progress might have been greater."

A man may be possessed of good ability and otherwise excellent qualities, but if he lacks application and industry, his chances of success will be very precarious, and this holds good, especially in mercantile life. In no occupation are indefatigable energy and close attention so indispensable to success as in that of the merchant, and if he is not willing, in this age of competition and push, to devote himself assiduously and energetically to his calling, he can hardly hope to accomplish great results. The merchant's life is not a path of roses. It means hard work day in and day out, and even though the more laborious part of the work can be delegated to others, his active presence during business hours is nevertheless requisite. Irregularity and negligence in the proprietor are contagious, and, unlike good qualities, spread readily to every employé, and to every department of his business. Constant personal superintendence and vigilance are required to keep the business up to its full tension, and to infuse into everyone connected with it that spirit of endeavor and individual effort which

APPLICATION AND INDUSTRY.   65

is essential to the attainment of the greatest success.

The man who would and who does succeed as a merchant is not the man who neglects his business to attend to the various sports that attract people generally. "Business before pleasure" is an inexorable law to him, and he who undertakes to reverse this order will surely reverse his business and his future.

It is the steady pull in one direction and constant watchfulness of your own particular business that is needed to succeed in mercantile life, and to keep fully posted on all the details of your business and its ever-varying status, requires more labor and attention than the average man comprehends, or if comprehending, is willing to bestow, even were ultimate success assured him. Men work hard without necessarily combining the quality of prolonged and steadfast application. They labor to get bread and butter, because they can not procure it without. But a capacity and willingness to work, coupled with application, signifies vastly more. It indicates both physical effort and will-power to accomplish a purpose, and this not only for direct and immediate gain, but for future benefits. Likewise, application means stick-to-itiveness, and trusting to the law of compensation for your reward, which is always sure to follow, provided the "bumps" of application and industry are not overshadowed by those of an antagonistic or neutralizing character. Very industrious people are sometimes known to make little or no headway financially, but to this we have simply to say, that man was given five distinct physical senses, and if we should find a man with only the sense of touch, though it be abnormally developed and cultivated, we should still pronounce him an imperfect creation, and so with the mental faculties. In temperaments, we cite the happy medium as our ideal. The individual to whom fortune has decreed a harmonious combination and co-ordination of all his faculties, to him has been given to enjoy the highest estate of man.

"Sammy, take care of your shop, and your shop will take care of you," was the advice of a Hebrew father to his son, and the admonition came from a competent source. Our Jewish brethren succeed in business, or anything else they undertake, to a much greater degree than any other class; but notice their methods. Causes have their effects, and industry its reward. Who works harder and devotes himself more closely and unwearingly to his calling? He not only keeps watch of every detail of his business, but he is always on hand to give it personal attention. He does not run his business by proxy.

Reports usually say "attentive to business," or "not attentive," with more or less details on the subject, as the case may be. Inattention to one's business is inexcusable, and is sufficient cause for lack of confidence—in fact, no man is entitled to credit who neglects his own business.

The business-man, in his function of creditor, can not afford to ignore so important a factor of strength or deficiency in his debtor, as application and industry.

BUSINESS EDUCATION.

In France, England, and other countries, commerce is classed among the sciences. Although it must of necessity be as much a science in this country as elsewhere, we have been content to let the science part take care of itself, while going in "on our muscle," and making all the money we can. But when we consider how little attention is paid in this country to business training, and how much time is devoted to other callings to fit our youth for active, intelligent work, the conviction is forced on us that we are lax in our appreciation of proper discipline.

Commerce rules the world to-day, and more people are engaged in it for their living than in all other callings combined. This being the case, and our individual and collective welfare being dependent on our efforts as businessmen, why should we or how can we afford to remain indifferent to the really practical part of our education?

To be sure, our boys start out in life by taking clerkships. These should be, properly, apprenticeships, and in some cases they serve that purpose; but with the large majority of cases they do not. The eagerness to get a dollar a week more is the all-absorbing ambition, and to stick to some one thing, and learn it thoroughly, is of secondary importance. As a rule, our boys start out to get "something to do," without thought on their part, or that of the parents, as to the selection of a permanent business to be followed throughout life.

The American boy is always on the alert for more money. As a quality in itself, it is commendable and essential if he selects commercial life for his vocation; but how much more effective would his efforts be, if his native genius were combined with correct discipline and methodical training?

The wise and well-meaning parent is anxious to secure a clerkship for his son in some old, reputable house, without especial reference to pay. He wants him not only to learn some particular branch of trade, but he is desirous that correct principles, along with the general routine of business, should be instilled into his mind.

In youth we are impressionable, and our faculties are equally susceptible to good or bad influences. Now and then we find even boys, who are a "law unto themselves" in their quick discrimination between right and wrong, good or bad, methods; but, as a rule, imitation is the most active faculty.

The youths of the Athenian age were subjected to the most rigorous training and discipline to make of them soldiers and warriors, and to fit them the better, they were educated as well in all the known branches of science. Thorough discipline of mind and body were carried to the extremes of hardship and privation. But in our day, commerce has superseded the art of war, and holds sway over all the world. The sword and the spear are converted into plowshares and other implements to be used by an army of wealth-producing artisans, instead of an army of bread-consuming idlers. The soldiers and warriors of the Athenian age have given place to the merchants and manufacturers of to-day, and why should not our fighting forces be as well equipped now as then?

The great question before the nations of the world in this generation, is that of commercial supremacy. Legislative enactments and political measures are devised for the development of our resources, and to facilitate the exchange of products, all with the view to our national growth and advancement, and for securing that supremacy for our own country. Considering, then, how momentous the question, not less, however, than the capacity and prestige of our competitors, if we would meet them successfully, we must bring to bear, not only our natural advantages, conditions, and aptitude, but we must raise these to their highest capabilities by training and cultivating our minds in that direction.

This article is confined to the merits of a

practical business education, and is not intended to enter the domain of education in general. Most of our business-men are self-educated. What degree of primary education should be necessary for a business-man to have, is outside the jurisdiction of this work. We have to do with business education and training only, in so far as it has any bearing on the subject of making credits.

The applicant for credit has either served an apprenticeship or has not. If he has not, he is still to serve, and in trusting him, we are trusting to the chance of his serving it to a purpose. If he has served his time, and acquired a knowledge of business, it is desirable to know how, where, and what were the surroundings and influences.

HONESTY.

We have here to do with honesty as we find it in our every-day business transactions with one another, and in thus confining the subject within these limits, we shall find that honesty is somewhat elastic. The moment we apply the moral law to it, the subject becomes more rigid and inflexible; but to measure our mercantile transactions in general by the moral standard, could not help being disastrous to many a fair business reputation. Our business affairs are governed by our civil laws, and each man can draw upon the moral law and be governed by it, additionally, as much as he pleases. The former exacts only conformity to the letter; the latter to the spirit; hence the man who pays his debts dollar for dollar, and discharges his obligations according to the letter, *must* be called honest. Our business code asks for nothing more, and how far he may fall short of the moral code, we leave for him to settle.

Shakespeare says: "To be an honest man is to be one in ten thousand." His measure must have been the moral law, for we can not think that commercial honesty, even in his day, was at such a fearful discount. That honesty is developed in man along with his other traits, and in the same ratio, must stand an admitted fact, otherwise our "philosophy of evolution," our ideas of human progress, would be wanting in their very essence.

Speaking from a commercial standpoint, and confining ourselves to those engaged in mercantile pursuits, we find them honest; i. e., with a liberal allowance for exceptions, as in other rules. The surprise is rather that people in trade or out of it are as honest as we find them, when we consider the fact that a man who is half-way sharp, can not alone be dishonest and succeed in defrauding his creditors and his friends, but he can evade the clutches of the law with equal success. What, then, tends to make men honest? In the first place, the quality is innate in man. The germ of honesty is in every civilized breast, though variously developed. Secondly, the quality of honesty finds compensation in its own exercise. Honesty has its reward, present and future, although it may not always come in the manner expected or most desired.

The world's experience, if not his own, has proven to the merchant that he can afford to be honest. He has no need to stifle that generous and manly impulse, for doing so, is more likely to strew his path with thorns than with roses. After a man has succeeded in gaining a competency, there is no longer any incentive to dishonesty, and he values the good opinion of his fellow-man quite as much as his possessions, and no reason exists for sacrificing either. On the other hand, the merchant who still has his mark to make, can by no force of reasoning afford to be dishonest, even though he were dead to all sense of honor. If men could engage in enterprises to-day, and to-morrow retire with sufficient spoils to make them reasonably independent for life, no doubt the temptation would prove too great for many a man who now struggles along, and will continue the struggle, as an honest man. But even this case is not derogatory to our faith in the innate and practical honesty of man. The temptation would assail those only whose character is too weak or whose desire for luxurious living is too great to resist it, and in either case it will simply prove that there was a lack of coôrdination of the mental faculties. Children are born deficient in their moral and mental, as well as physical, organizations sometimes, and that we find occasionally a conscienceless, unscrupulous member of society, must be accepted in the light of other phenomena, and as forming the exception, and not the rule.

"Honesty is the best policy," is a truism, the force of which we all appreciate as a gospel truth, whether we have been honest or not. The dishonest man believes it, though he can not speak from his own experience. He probably does so, however, from observation and by comparison. Perhaps the most convincing proof of the correctness of the maxim was given by an old merchant on retiring from business. He was giving his farewell advice to a young man who had served him faithfully, and in whom he had taken a deep interest. He concluded by saying: "My son, let me repeat to you that honesty is the best policy. I have tried both ways, and I know." Here was a man who was willing to acknowledge that he had tried both ways, and by actual experiment had found that the adage was true.

I find in the *Bankers' Monthly* for October, in an address delivered by Mr. L. J. Gage, of the First National Bank, of Chicago, the following axiom laid down: "All good men love the approval of the good, and all bad men are held in check in fear of the good man's reproach." The fundamental principles enunciated here bear out the argument that man naturally leans toward truth and honesty and against their opposites.

Integrity is the rock on which the vast commercial interests of the world are resting for their foundation. Annihilate that, and we destroy trade and commerce, and in the train of its destruction will follow civilization and all the benefits arising out of it. Without faith and confidence in each other's honesty there can be no credit, and without credit very little business.

To be honest, to do your duty toward yourself and your neighbor, is not a specially meritorious act. An obligation or a duty is discharged with its conscientious performance, and that simply ends it as it ought to end. But the failure to perform the duty, the act of being dishonest, for this there can be no excuse on either moral or business grounds.

If your applicant for credit can not show a clean record as regards honesty, let him apply somewhere else. You can not afford to take any chances on him. Even where we act most advisedly, the percentage of loss is large enough without taking extra hazardous risks.

ECONOMY.

With every advantage of capital, ability, and prestige, a merchant's ultimate and permanent success would still be a matter of doubt if he did not combine economy with his other good qualities and advantages. Extravagance is the cause of innumerable commercial wrecks; it is the reef on which many a good craft founders. Extravagance, in the sense used here, has a wide range. A man may spend $50,000 a year and yet not be prodigal; whereas, another would not be warranted in spending $2,000, or even $1,000. This depends entirely on a man's income, and what portion of it is assured beyond all reasonable doubt.

All fortunes, the largest not excepted, accumulated in mercantile pursuits, or, we might say, in any pursuit, are the result of strict economy, and this applies to personal, as well as business, expenses. You can not have the golden eggs and eat the goose that lays them. The experiment has been, and always will be tried, but it will never be attended with success. In summing up the lives of our eminent merchants we shall always find, underlying and combined with other sterling qualities, that cardinal quality of economy, and how far this constitutes a factor in their success, I will endeavor to show.

The poor man, and even the moderately successful, envies the prosperous and wealthy merchant, and fails to see any present indications of economy in the latter's method or manner of living. He fails to see where economy cuts any figure, and, looked at from a present standpoint, the merchant certainly does not appear to deny himself any pleasure or comfort that money can buy or heart can wish; but economy, nevertheless, is the main factor in bringing about the difference in circumstances between him and his less-favored brother. Causes have their effects. We look at the wealthy merchant of to-day and see riches and independence, but these are only legitimate results of a first cause, and though the cause is remote from our point of observation, and is lost sight of, it nevertheless has existence, and we want to make sure of this fact. It is safe to say that the merchant, whom so many envy, would never have become an object of envy unless he had possessed the quality of practical economy in his make-up at a time when it was requisite, and when, to build a solid foundation, it was necessary to practice self-denial and make every cent available as working capital.

The men who do the envying would rarely have been willing, under similar or any circumstances, to have suffered the voluntary privations and hardships which all self-made and successful men have endured. The early struggles of all merchants, who have amassed fortunes and built up colossal enterprises, read much the same, and in many cases their early habits of personal economy and simplicity are retained long after the need exists for counting the pennies.

Man as a free agent has full control over the exercise of this faculty, and to practice frugality and self-denial is a voluntary act. To practice economy when compulsory, can not be designated a virtue. It is a virtue only when man's will-power is exercised in the direction of voluntarily renouncing present comforts for the accomplishment of a future object; that is, eventual success and independence.

Some writer has said that economy is the parent of liberty and ease. The purpose of going into business, primarily, is to make a living and to provide for our daily wants, and the majority of people in trade make no more. It is even questionable if they make that, when we consider how much money is annually contributed through failures, and this certainly goes toward the maintenance of those who have not succeeded in making a living in their respective callings. Simultaneously with the merchant's desire to make a living comes the ambition to make something more, to store up the fruits of his labors for his declining years and for the dependent ones. Eventual liberty and ease are the motives; but this desire, innate though it be in our civilized communities, can only become an accomplished fact under favorable conditions, and when the fundamental requirements of trade are complied with. That they are not, is proven by our trade statistics.

We know, for a fact, that consumers will buy more when they can do so on credit than when they have to pay cash, or have made it a rule with themselves to buy only for cash. With the dealer the temptation has a double potency. For his personal wants and indulgence, he has both money and merchandise under his immediate control, though he may be indebted for both, and not even a formal request for credit is necessary. He simply takes what he wants and uses it as he sees fit. When his own and his creditor's property is consumed, we have the announcement of a failure. When we consider, then, the ease with which wants can be gratified, and compare it with man's capacity, or rather incapacity, to resist temptation, the smallness of the number of successful businessmen is no surprise. If the practice of economy were a universal trait, there would be less pauperism and poverty. It is the opposite trait in man, however, that prevails. Profligacy and extravagance are the causes that disturb individuals and society.

For practical illustrations of what economy, or the want of it, will accomplish, it is only necessary for the reader to look back, say twenty-five years, and recall the houses in business, and see how many, or rather how few, have survived till the present time. There must be reasons for this, and a careful examination will reveal them. It will be found invariably that the survivors have been of the careful, conservative, and rigidly economical class. They haven't made haste, neither have they made waste. Of a certain twenty-five large houses doing business twenty-five years ago, I find to-day but two in existence. Personal acquaintance with the business methods of all these houses leads to but one verdict. It was simply a question of economy versus extravagance and careless management. The man who is economical is always careful.

Money put out at interest accumulates fast. Invested in business, money is calculated to, and should, bring a larger return than ordinary interest. Judging from the past ten years, a dollar kept in business and allowed to accumulate, should double in about six years. Now, as an illustration, we will take two houses: "A" draws $4,000 for his expenses; "B" $8,000. In ten years behold the difference in their relative financial conditions, all other things being conducted equally favorably. "A's" savings of $4,000 per year over "B" will give the former, at the end of ten years, about $80,000 excess capital. This $80,000 and its compound accumulations of profit, if retained in the business another ten years, will constitute in itself an independent fortune. I make this calculation simply to give a cursory glance at what saving and economy will do, when put to a practical and mathematical test; and these figures don't lie; they apply in all cases.

The great difficulty with man is, that his wants are more progressive than his income. To make our business and our profits increase is a difficulty out of all proportion to the facility with which we increase our wants and expenses. It takes more determination and will-power to preserve the equilibrium between these two factors than the average man possesses, and herein lies, largely, the cause of failure among business-men.

To the merchant, then, about to extend credit, the question of economy is of paramount importance, since the applicant's success and our safety depend largely on this one factor.

MARRIED OR SINGLE.

It might seem that whether a man was married or single, could have no pertinency to the question at issue, and that it could hardly constitute a factor in our consideration of his claim to credit. But a man's social status does have a bearing on the subject, both present and remote; and while we may be neglectful of its importance in many cases, it does not signify that we can really afford to be so.

The words credit and trust are, in a sense, synonymous terms. We necessarily place trust in a man who gets credit from us. We trust to his honesty or responsibility, or to legal redress, to enforce the fulfillment of his contract; otherwise, we should never extend credit to any man. We have confidence in a man to trust him with our goods or money, and we are his creditors; or he may have our confidence as employers for a place of trust as agent or employé. Either case is one of trust, pure and simple.

Now, it will be found that in applying to a house for a position of trust, one of the leading questions asked will be if you are married or single; and the question is not an impertinent one, or asked out of mere curiosity. All things being equal, the man with family will have the preference; and the reason for it is founded on the presumption that the latter, owing to his family ties and domestic responsibility, is considered more in the light of a permanent fixture, more settled, and is credited with a greater degree of stability. The single man, on the other hand, without family ties and considerations, and who has no one's welfare to consider, and no reputation and character to injure but his own, is undoubtedly more prone to questionable habits and is an easier prey to temptations. If some irregularity, either premeditated or otherwise, imperil his safety, there is nothing to hinder him from getting out of the law's reach on short notice.

This is the way, at any rate, in which the case is summed up, though oftentimes quite unconsciously.

The cases of a trusted employé or agent and that of a debtor, are identical, and the argument will apply with equal force to both.

No claim is made here of greater honesty of the one over the other. The innate honesty of both is precisely the same, but difference in conditions and surroundings is liable to cause different actions and ambitions. The married state with a man favors personal economy, concentration of effort to a purpose, the mainspring of that purpose being the comfort and welfare of his family. We furthermore recognize as a fact, that if a man in business be a married man, he has a greater incentive to apply himself more closely to business and to devote all his energy and ability to his success. Our whole social and commercial fabric is based on the individual effort and desire of each man to raise his family to the highest degree of respectability and independence.

AGE.

The age of a man, if he is about to be your debtor, is *not* an unimportant factor in determining his claim to credit. Our dependence is not alone on ability, honesty, and other elements, but we rely, from the nature of things, on energy, ambition, and large combativeness. These qualities in the aged or infirm are on the wane, and in the very youthful business-man are often, we might say generally, misdirected for want of experience. After a man has passed the prime of life our confidence decreases in the ratio of his advancing years, and consequent decline of vitality and active usefulness. This, of course, only applies to cases where men past their prime engage in new undertakings, or who have struggled unsuccessfully up to late in life without gaining a firm footing. The latter form quite a numerous class.

For an aged man to engage actively in business for a livelihood is to us an admission, unconsciously, perhaps, that thus far his mercantile career has been a failure; and taking the past and best part of his life as a criterion, what can be the reasonable expectation for future success when pitted against younger men, keen competitors, and newer methods? And, on this question of different methods, it is a fact that, though the ways of doing things change, men do not change with the changing methods. Men accustomed to the ways and methods of doing business fifty years ago could not become reconciled to our way. There is a limit to man's tenure of progressiveness, and that once passed, he either becomes passive or obstructive. But, fortunately for the world, the wane of energy and combativeness resulting from age induces passiveness, and permits younger men and the genius of succeeding generations to build on the foundations laid by our seniors. All things in this world are wisely arranged to the end that man's progressiveness and development may not be retarded.

The argument that the credit-man would naturally use with reference to a would-be debtor, past the prime of life, would be based on the possibility of failure and the chances of securing his account after that. This case would present little encouragement. The chances of recovery, and subsequent ability to pay, can hardly be considered. With a young or middle-aged man, however, we feel that his tenure of life is long enough, so that a judgment may eventually be good; or at any rate, we may choose to compromise and let him continue, and thus recover our loss indirectly through his future patronage. In the latter case we feel justified in speculating on the possibilities of the future, which we are denied in the former.

Extreme youth also needs consideration, and

makes our chances equally precarious, though for different reasons. A very young man, if he fails, seldom sticks to the ship. He either feels that he has had quite enough experience in the line he was engaged in, or knows just enough to know that he has mistaken his calling, and in either case he generally seeks employment for which he thinks he is better adapted. Generally, he is lost sight of by his old creditors and those interested in his first business venture, and by the time he gets ready to embark in business again, old claims against him are forgotten or outlawed.

The experience of all business-men is corroborative of these statements concerning the extremes of youth and age, and the credit-man should take full cognizance of them.

CAPITAL.

We have thus far dwelt on the importance of things which in themselves would not pay bills. We *can not* take five dollars' worth of experience or of ability and use it as collateral, or as an equivalent to money value. We can, however, use our experience and ability in such manner as will produce the five dollars, and with the proceeds pay the debt.

The man who loans you his property—that is to say, trusts you with his goods—does so with the belief that their value will be augmented by the aid of your experience, ability, and labor. Absolute confidence in your integrity are the conditions of such a credit, but, in the generality of cases, the creditor would also require, for his safety, a proportion of capital, to be furnished by you, and the larger that proportion of capital is to the credit asked, the better it is for both debtor and creditor.

If all men paid spot-cash for all they bought, there would be no need of questioning their ability, honesty, or anything else. Trade distinguishes between neither race, color, nor religion.

The amount of capital required in any given case to insure safety and success, is an uncertain quantity, ranging from 0 to 100. Some men have the faculty of making money, or rather of accumulating it, under the most unfavorable circumstances, while others, even more favorably situated, can never make both ends meet.

In the customer, therefore, asking credit, we have to consider all the elements that go to make up a good business-man, and let the capital be the last consideration instead of the first; though it would seem that so important a factor as capital, should be the primary consideration. As we find business conducted, it must stand as an admitted fact, that few houses—wholesale, retail, or manufacturing—restrict their business to a basis of their cash capital. We may safely calculate that nine out of ten could not do sufficient business to make it profitable were they limited to this in their transactions. What they use in lieu of capital, is confidence, and as long as they succeed in holding this, they can continue and prosper. The point desired to be made, is, that the capital *ordinarily* controlled by a dealer is not sufficient without he also has the confidence of the community. Therefore, when he suffers this to be lost by any unfortunate or questionable maneuver, his resources are crippled, and his chances must thereafter be ranked doubtful. Capital and confidence are deserving of the motto: "United we stand, divided we *fail*."

Of capital itself, one of the most important things to know, is how its owner came into possession of it.

(1) If, as a clerk, he has been gaining experience and education, and by dint of economy and frugal habits has accumulated a capital with which he proposes to do business on his own account, every dollar of that man's capital has an enhanced value. In the first place, he has shown ability to earn, and frugality to save, and having both earned and saved, he knows the value of money as no man can who has done neither. This man may be regarded as good for any reasonable business wants, and is entitled to our confidence.

(2) If the money was inherited by a young man, or he in any way came into possession of it without effort on his own part, and he uses it to engage in business, it will then depend entirely on how much natural ability and experience he combines with his capital. Without an established reputation as to his business qualifications, his capital would be all there is to base credit on; hence, we could only trust him with safety to the extent of his bank account. Acquiring the needful experience and education should always precede the employment of capital, but where the education and experience are undertaken to be gained concurrently with the use of capital, there is always danger that the latter will be lost before the former is gained.

(3) Cases that frequently come up are, where a young man without experience, and

with next to no ability, usually, is started by some well-to-do relative, father, mother, uncle, or aunt. There is said to be no end of money behind the young man, but, as experience proves, the end of the money is seldom very long in being reached. This class is not very difficult to handle for the credit-man. It is generally only a question of time when the aforesaid relatives become solicitous about the business and its success, and they must be secured, and it is usually understood in the beginning that they shall not lose by the venture, no matter who else loses. Of course, the general creditor "gets left." Experience teaches that credit must here be confined within very narrow limits.

(4) To engage in mercantile pursuits, men do not have to go through a preparatory routine of study or of apprenticeship, like the professional man or the man with a trade. A man can not be a doctor to-day and a lawyer to-morrow, or a shoemaker one day and a tailor the next; but either of them can turn merchant at any time. Men leave professions, trades, farms, etc., every day and enter into business regardless of previous training, or go from one kind of business to another, as if to be a merchant was an inborn attribute of every man.

To formulate a rule by which to pass judgment on this heterogeneous tribe, or rather this "job lot," would be impossible. Applications for credit in these cases should be governed by the record of previous business connections and conduct, and that these are obtained is most essential. This will furnish valuable data for the credit-man, and may or may not, in his opinion, entitle the applicant to credit. But in the absence of any such data, the applicant's claim to credit can only be considered on the basis of his cash capital, and the future must establish his claim to increased confidence.

The further consideration of capital will be taken up again under the head of "Limit of Credit."

ASSETS: STOCK AND PERSONAL PROPERTY.

We have reference here, of course, to that portion of the assets of an insolvent concern, which consists of merchantable wares or goods. The term merchandise is understood to mean articles of commerce in general demand, or wares that have ready sale. When we have to do, therefore, with merchandise assets, to be closed out and converted into cash, we may generally and reasonably expect to realize somewhere near the original cost price, provided that the goods were bought judiciously, and provided a market exists where disposition of them must be made. Ordinarily this class of assets is the most available to the creditor, and brings more nearly face value than any other, though even here the shrinkage is always considerable, not, however, from lack of representative market value, but for reasons outside.

An assignee's sale, according to the manner in which such sales are usually made and allowed to drag, always involves large expense for clerk hire, rent, and incidental items, besides legal services, etc. If closed out by piece-meal the expenses will be out of all proportion to the receipts, and the net proceeds will be equally impaired. If sold in a lump for cash, the buyer usually names his own terms, and in both instances the creditor fares about alike, only that the latter method is the best, because it is the quickest, by avoiding contingencies in allowing returns to be made to those interested.

From this it will be seen that in case of liquidation by assignee's sale, even the most available portion of a bankrupt's assets will undergo considerable shrinkage before it is converted into cash and ready to divide, and that 35 per cent. loss on the appraised market value (leaving the creditors 65 per cent.) is only a fair average discount.

In calculating, then, the value of a dealer's stock in trade as part representative of his capital, we are not warranted in estimating it at over 65 per cent. on the purported inventory value, when a credit is in contemplation. In few cases will this figure be exceeded, and in many cases it will not be reached. In making credits, the possibility of a failure should always be borne in mind, and our estimates of property, to be safe, must be based on that contingency.

In respect to manufacturing business, we must allow ourselves even greater latitude for shrinkage of assets. A large portion of the assets will necessarily be represented by stock in various stages of completion at all times, and which, consequently have no market value. In the event of failure, this class of assets could only be converted at great sacrifice of material and labor expended thereon, and they possess really less commercial value than the raw material out of which they are made. We can give them only a nominal value.

Next comes the stock of manufactured goods. The ready conversion of these into cash will depend on the nature of the goods. What they may bring in the open market and at forced sale, is governed by circumstances. If the product happens to be of a seasonable kind, then it must be sold in its season to realize the most, and if sale is forced out of season, the sacrifice will be proportionately large. The raw material, on the other hand, represents and commands more nearly market value, and can in nearly all cases be readily disposed of, even more so than the manufactured product itself.

But the assets of a manufacturing concern that represent the least value at forced sale are those consisting of the plant, so-called; i. e., the machinery, tools, fixtures, patterns, etc. This class of property, if sold at any time, will bring only second-hand prices, and if closed out by an assignee, only a small percentage of the original cost is realized. The creditors have little to hope for from this source in the way of addition to their dividend. What represents thousands of dollars, will scarcely realize as many hundreds. For this reason manufacturing concerns generally effect a settlement on their own terms. The creditors do not want to carry on the business; it can not be sold at anything near its actual value, and so the owners are the most desirable parties to keep and continue to operate it on whatever reasonable terms they choose to name. They can, in fact, afford to pay more for it than outside parties.

The assets of a merchant's stock in trade being worth about 65 per cent., that of a manufacturer can not be estimated at more than 35 per cent., if closed out for the benefit of the creditors; and in making credits we must discriminate, therefore, between the different branches of business, and duly consider the nature of the assets.

ASSETS: ACCOUNTS AND BILLS RECEIVABLE.

It is anything but amusing to a creditor to read an assignee's report of the condition of a defunct concern, when that official states with cold-blooded disinterestedness, that of the $5,000 due the insolvent in accounts and notes, only about $1,000 is collectible. What a picnic the dead-beats in the bankrupt's locality must have had, and what a generous, accommodating merchant he must have been! Generous man, surely—to all but himself and those who undertook to help him. And such instances are not rare, by any means. Far worse come under our notice repeatedly, and we resign ourselves with stolid indifference as to the outcome.

Ordinarily, however, this class of assets will bring as much as merchandise, viz., about 65 per cent. net. Accounts and notes do not cost as much to collect, as goods do to convert into cash. There is neither rent, clerk-hire, nor any of the other expenses incident to carrying and disposing of a stock of goods and personal property, and if the insolvent has used moderately good judgment, the shrinkage on their face value may be calculated not to exceed 35 per cent. In the hands of the owner they would be worth considerably more, for the

ASSETS: ACCOUNTS AND BILLS RECEIVABLE. 99

reason that debtors of a bankrupt concern are never eager to pay, and in fact, will use every means to evade even just debts. The assignee's or receiver's task is, therefore, made difficult and expensive, and a large portion of the accounts is usually absorbed in legal fees and costs.

It is safe to assume that men always engage in business where their capital can find employment to its full extent. A man with $1,000 capital generally undertakes to do a business where twice that sum would be needed, for comfort and ease. He calculates on the time he has to give; that is, bases his calculations on the terms nominally established in his trade. If the calculation is made to hold good, and he is firmly resolved to do his credit business without swerving from his purpose, he is all right. But very few have the nerve to do this, and fewer still appreciate the importance of limiting their credit-giving.

The ignorance on this question is often seen in merchants, who seem to think that if they pay interest on past-due accounts, that they are fulfilling all the obligations as between debtor and creditor. No merchant can afford to loan any portion of his working capital for simple interest. In order to make it pay, he must turn his capital many times in a year. To loan it out at 6 per cent. means simply getting 6 per cent. per annum. Let any merchant undertake to pay all the expenses of doing business for a return of only 6 per cent. on his capital once a year, and he will very soon have no capital. And what holds good when taken on a large scale, holds equally good on a smaller.

As to the importance of strict adherence to your terms, and insisting that they shall be lived up to on the part of your customers, the following simple illustration will suffice: If a merchant has a capital which enables him to give sixty days' time and still discount his bills, does it cut any figure or interfere with his discounting his bills, should he be compelled to give ninety days? Most certainly it would. He would have tied up additional capital, equal to thirty days' sales, which would not be available to him in time to discount his own bills any longer. The longer the time that is given or allowed to be taken, the greater will be the proportion of our capital made unavailable. Large and first-class houses understand this, and we have always found them demanding punctuality in the observance of terms. A firm doing a business of $1,000,000 per month, for instance, if it gives sixty days' time, means that $2,000,000 are owing it, and ninety days' would mean $3,000,000 outstanding. Of course, more or less of our sales are discounted, but this we anticipate in our calculations here as well as in practice.

ASSETS: ACCOUNTS AND BILLS RECEIVABLE. 101

Whether we undertake to discount our bills for cash or buy on time, it will be seen that our safety, comfort, and reputation for promptness, depend very much on the relative proportions of accounts and bills receivable to our capital. A man with $10 doing a C. O. D. business, can turn his capital every day in the year if buyers can be found. Making 10 per cent. profit on each turn, that $10 would earn over $300 per year, supposing that the daily profit was put aside. That same man, if he sold his $10 worth of goods on six months' time, could only turn his capital twice a year, and he would make only twice 10 per cent. on $10.

This treatise will not permit of additional argument on this subject, but we can not allow the opportunity to pass without calling special attention to its importance as a prominent factor in the science of credits.

Giving indefinite time and carrying your customers as long as they desire, at interest, is being done successfully and profitably by merchants sometimes, and they are shrewd merchants. But they are men who have sufficient capital to carry on both mercantile and banking business, and can conduct the one conjointly with, but independently of, the other. The merchant turns banker every three or six months, and gets his accounts secured and drawing good interest. He could use his banking or surplus capital in no more profitable or safer way. He furthermore ties these men to him, and as long as they owe him and he wants their patronage, he need not fear competition.

But this class of merchants are the exception. The great mass we have do with lack the capital, and some also the brains, to do one business comfortably and as it should be done.

REAL ESTATE—EXEMPTIONS.

Real estate and permanent improvements should offer the very best basis for credit, and they do, when clear and unincumbered. But very few merchants, comparatively, hold property in fee simple. There is nearly always an incumbrance on it, large or small, but always large enough to make the property unavailable for the general creditor in case of insolvency. Even when the property is scheduled as clear at a given time, the owner usually raises money on it before an assignment is made, sometimes with the expectation of tiding over, and sometimes to save it from the wreck; but as creditors are not inclined to advance more money in order to control the debtor's equity, the result is that whatever sum that equity may represent, it is seldom convertible or available as an asset for the benefit of the creditors.

There is this good feature with real estate, however, as part of the representative capital: It can not be transferred without giving immediate notice to the public. The records, as are those of the chattel mortgage, are closely watched by the mercantile agency reporters for the benefit of creditors, and whether conveyed for legitimate or fraudulent purposes, the community is, in either case, advised of the fact.

A homestead is exempt. The Homestead law in various States places different limits on the value that may be claimed as exempt, but there is a wide latitude allowed usually in the appraisal, and practically the creditor's equity in it is never tangible. The value, whatever it may be, can not, therefore, be considered as part of the working and available capital of the business. It adds to a man's credit in this, that it makes him more of a fixture, and enables him to live more economically to the extent that he saves paying rent.

In new States and Territories the laws are particularly favorable to the people in them, and the exemptions warrantable under the statutes give the debtor class all the advantage. For the creditor there exists no legal jurisdiction, and practically he is more dependent on the honor and honesty of his customers than he is on the exercise of any legal rights that he ought justly be allowed to claim; but notwithstanding this fact, and in spite of the insecurity, so far as a property basis is concerned, credit to those localities does not seem to suffer material restriction.

The credit-man is sometimes misled by the scheduling, on the part of his customer, of store-building as part of his capital, when in fact it is used conjointly for business and *dwelling* purposes, which brings it under the head of exemptions and the Homestead law.

These points are important, and a thorough knowledge of the nature of the property, either real or personal, is indispensable in order to reasonably insure our safety as creditors.

The business code of fifty years ago required of a debtor, who made any pretense to honesty and honorable conduct, that he turn over every dollar's worth of property, without reference to legal exemptions whatever, in liquidation of his debts. A man was considered dishonest who kept back anything whatsoever; but this code has given place to a more modern and extenuating one. The unfortunate's family is considered to be entitled to a home, if one is owned, and the commercial ethics of the present day sanction its exemption as a debt-paying factor. The family, in particular, is a gainer by the operation of these ethics, and society at large is relieved of a possible burden. From the standpoint of commercial ethics of the present time, the bankrupt is accorded not only a legal, but a moral, right to provide a home for his wife and children and keep them in the enjoyment of it, and the sentiment, while it may be abused frequently, is both charitable and humane, and in harmony and accord with our sense of national and individual independence.

LIABILITIES.

ACCOUNTS AND BILLS PAYABLE IN PROPORTION TO CAPITAL.

Things must always bear relative proportions to each other to insure safety of the whole. This holds as good in carrying on and building up a business, as in the construction of a house. In the chapter on the "Limit of Credit," on page 171, we have discussed the question of how much a business can safely owe in proportion to its assets, from the standpoint of the creditor. To suppose a case of a merchant whose liabilities are equal to his assets, is practically admitting a clear case of insolvency into our argument, and a case without capital. This is a hopeless case, but such cases are not nearly as rare as they might be, and sometimes they even enjoy good credit and unbounded confidence. But there is always an end. The staving-off process works for a while, and accommodating creditors remain patient beyond the limits of prudence. At last, when endurance has ceased to be a virtue, and the debt must be paid, and neither extension of time nor further credit for goods can be obtained, the culminating point is reached, and we are glad to take, in a case of this kind, 50 cents on the dollar, and call ourselves lucky at that. In fact, 50 cents is quite a princely offer.

Liabilities have the faculty of growing day and night without our aid, while the assets of a debtor who is hard up and behind, acquire just the reverse attribute. Instead of growing in value, they diminish from day to day. The reason of this is obvious.

The man who keeps his liabilities within proper limits; i. e., within the limits of absolute safety to his own business, enjoys advantages, by reason of his good standing, which he can always turn to profit. To the man, on the other hand, who is too much in debt already, no one has any bargains to offer. He pays outside prices for everything, and his competitors get the bargains. The distance between him and his more fortunate neighbors is constantly widened, and their relative conditions may be seen in the prosperity of the one, and the growing distress of the other.

The man whose liabilities are out of proportion to his capital and business, and who is therefore constantly harassed to meet them, also suffers injury from more remote causes than from loss of confidence and credit. The constant worry attendant upon this condition, the efforts made to turn a corner here and there, the figuring and conniving required to pull through, all these things engage his mind and time, and withdraw his labor from its legitimate functions. A certain portion of services that a business-man has to perform are an expense or a loss; i. e., they are not productive. The salesman renders productive service, while that of the man employed to collect the bills is not productive. This belongs to the item of expense. If the bill had been paid in cash when the sale was made, no collector would have been necessary. Every time you send a man out to collect, it costs something, and whatever time is devoted, in a business way, to yesterday's transactions, is lost. If you made $1,000 last week on the sale of goods, it will never be more, and you can never make it more by any method of figuring; the more time you spend, and the more assistance you require to get possession of it, the less you will eventually realize. Now, the man who is in financial distress, *per force*, wastes a large portion of his time in unproductive efforts, although they may enable him to turn one more corner. But in no sense can it be contended that he has made or earned anything or added to his capital.

It is surprising with what rare persistence men hold on long after their condition is past hope. Micawber like, they are always waiting for something to turn up to help them out of their difficulties. When the collapse finally comes, as come it must, all are agreed that it would have been much better if it had come sooner. The creditor has lost money by the delay, and the debtor has lost time.

No definite rule can be laid down to govern the proper proportion of liabilities to assets and capital. We might approximate to this in some one line of business, but we are here concerned with business in general, including all branches. All we can say is this: Keep the mastership of your business in your own hands, and this you can do by keeping your indebtedness and your engagements within the limits of your positive ability to meet. The man who does this, merits and is entitled to our confidence; the man who does not, justly lays himself open to suspicion of jeopardizing, not alone his own capital, but ours as well.

VOLUME OF BUSINESS IN PROPORTION TO CAPITAL.

This question we can discuss only in a general way, and the considerations will be such as past experience and observation lead us to take cognizance of. No fault can be found with us, as a mercantile community, on the score of not doing business enough on the amount of our capital. The fault is rather that we attempt too much.

The function of money is to facilitate exchanges of our produce, and that a dollar in the hands of our business people is made to perform that function to its utmost capacity, we have no reason to question. Rust or moth does not get into our dollars or our capital, for it does not remain long enough in one place to become settled, and this is all very well as long as the dollar is kept moving and no unusual conditions arise. In that case, the person paying it out, and the party receiving it, each, in turn, is benefited. If nothing ever occurred to check the circulation of money at some given point, then we might rightfully claim that that method subserved the highest purpose which gives it the largest use in effecting exchanges, either for past or present transactions. Exchanges are made, i. e., goods are bought and sold on the basis that there is to be profit in the operations; therefore, the more transactions or trades that a dollar enables us to make, the more productive it becomes, and the greater the number of people that are benefited. But we find by experience, that when money reaches the point where the maximum number of operations are effected with it, and when exchanges are made with the greatest facility, and apparently with the least friction, which condition is indicative of universal and unlimited confidence in each other's ability to perform them, invariably a halt may be looked for which will shake our commercial structure and all our calculations to its very center. This is the panic. Every man who has passed through one or more commercial crises in this or other countries, if he has been at all observant, has noticed that financial distress to a community is always foreshadowed by excessive confidence, and an abnormal tendency to speculation. The limit of the purchasing power of a dollar is exceeded and ignored, and "promises to pay" take its place largely; and along the whole line each depends on the other for the fulfillment of promises, without any really tangible basis. They are notes without security, and the maker pays them *if he can*.

In the nature of things, in the buoyancy of our spirits and the sanguineness of our make-up as a business people, even the more conservative element loses its equilibrium during periods of apparently universal prosperity and confidence, to wake up at last and see the bubble burst, as burst it must, from its own over-inflation. The greed for gain is too strong to be resisted, and even our personal experiences do not seem to profit us. Inflexible laws govern our commercial transactions, as all else, and we should not be unmindful of indications or ignore the timely warnings that are always given and followed by the wary.

Whether a policy of safety and conservatism is the most profitable in the long run or not, is demonstrable by facts, and we can find our proofs by pointing to houses which have pursued this policy, and to the wrecks that are strewn all along the shore by following the opposite course. This is a practical test, and we need no better.

Panics do not come and go with the regularity of the moon's phases; but they come, nevertheless, in cycles, and there is a periodicity about them which the world is prone to overlook. The same, or similar, causes that led to the panic of 1857 and subsequent panics, will cause others, and the great majority of us will be caught in them, as if the records of preceding disasters had been completely destroyed.

The deductions we would make are based on the experience behind us and the probabilities before us. The former enables us, as wise business-men, to establish a scientific basis by

BUSINESS IN PROPORTION TO CAPITAL. 113

which to govern our actions with reference to the probabilities in the future. Conditions, relations, and confidences must be looked at in the light of cause and effect, and the good business-man anticipates the effect long before it is produced. There is science in business, notwithstanding that this fact has not dawned upon the multitude. A hap-hazard method is always conditioned upon the whims of chance, and success is not its legitimate offspring.

What amount of business a man can safely do with a given capital would be as difficult to determine, in an abstract way, as to determine the chances of success of a new enterprise without a knowledge of the necessary facts and surrounding conditions. We know, as experienced credit-men, that when a concern does so much business that it can not pay its bills promptly, it is not safe to extend credit to it. Over-buying, over-trading, and not the least, over-trusting, are the greatest evils we have to contend with. The only rule that can be laid down to guide us safely, is to do all the business we can, but stop short of the point where the *fulfillment of our promises* is dependent upon the strict observance of the promises of others to us.

In other words, we must keep ourselves in condition to meet our obligations, whether others meet theirs or not. A merchant is not compelled, by this rule, to have the cash in bank at all times for all his debts. That is not necessary. A certain percentage of accounts and assets can always be relied on and realized from. The liabilities should be kept within the limit of this percentage, leaving the balance as a surplus, or as the representative of capital invested.

ANTECEDENTS.

A man's antecedents are found in his written and unwritten biography. Like a barometer, they unerringly indicate and give us an idea of his character, ability, honesty; his good and bad traits, and summing up, we are in possession of valuable data for judging his future, and our chances, if thrown with him.

Because a man has once failed in business is nothing in itself, in this country, at least. A man may come out of a wreck an honest, capable, and very often a better, man, by reason of his experience. Force of circumstances, joined to a little inexperience and imprudence, may have resulted in his bankruptcy; but in a case of this kind, where the integrity of the party has been kept inviolate, the business community is ever ready to overlook past mistakes, and bestow upon him its confidence in the future. But the case must be a clear one, and his integrity must stand out uncompromisingly; it must be "net, and no discount." Where such are the facts, reasonable hope of eventual recovery may be rightfully entertained, and our support be extended.

On the other hand, where the failure is the result of gross violation of business principles and honesty, as is often the case, the bankrupt should forever forfeit all claims on the confidence of the community, and were this more universally adhered to, a wholesome influence would be exerted on all classes.

Inexperience being largely the cause of many men's downfall in early life, there being no other blemish on their characters, the business world is always ready to forgive and help them again. Our charitableness toward the honest unfortunate is a grand feature in our modern mercantile life, and although it is actuated by policy and self-interest, that need not detract from its merits. A broad Christian sentiment underlies it withal.

There is a tendency to make light of failures by both the creditor and the bankrupt. The bankrupt thinks he will do better in the future, and, profiting by experience, will soon be enabled to get on his feet again—better than ever. But he counts without his host. Excepting the out-and-out thief, men are not benefited by their own failures. Although the debtor finds, usually, no difficulty in compromising with his creditors on a reasonable basis, such as the assets warrant, thus enabling him to continue his business; yet, of the majority it may be said, that their entire future is blighted, and that they never recover.

To a few, failure gives additional zest, and it would seem that it was the key to subsequent brilliant success, but we think the failure might have been omitted without peril to their final outcome. Failure always means a setback and loss of time, also loss of confidence, and the latter can only be regained in the course of time. Going along safely and cautiously, though somewhat slower, and avoiding failure, is assuredly the shortest road, after all, to success, and the attainment of our desires.

The time allotted to a man in business for permanently establishing himself, and gaining an undisputed foothold, is limited to but few years—thirty, at most, and this does not admit of many or any serious drawbacks. The time is too short, and most men find it so.

We like to see men ambitious and energetic. These are characteristics of our people. We make haste to get rich; but whether our undue haste does not lay waste a large portion of our efforts, and result in irretrievable loss of time, is a matter for serious consideration. Less haste to accomplish our purposes as businessmen, more conservatism and caution, would certainly advance the interest of trade and traders at large.

The applicant for credit favors, if he has ever failed, or whatever his past life may have been, has left a biography of himself that must be carefully read. All the facts will be enumerated therein, and will indicate to the credit-man the course he should pursue.

COMPETITION.

With the growth of population in every direction, east, west, north, and south, opportunities are opened up for business ventures, and as fast as a town or village is located, two stores are ready to start where only one is really needed. We are accumulating capital very fast, and there is no nook or corner anywhere, in the remotest part of this continent, that does not exert a magnetic influence on capital the moment a chance for its employment is offered. There is no enterprise so large that it can not be capitalized, or so small that it does not attract men to it with the hope of making a living.

The man with energy, experience, and a little capital, who drives his stakes first in any new town—the so-called pioneer—has considerable advantage, and his prestige makes it more difficult for others to get a foothold.

Every new town is always going to be *the* town, and in the expectation that it will outstrip every other, more stores are generally started than can find profitable remuneration. Of course, the law of supply and demand regulates this in due course of time, and only the fittest survive.

Competition is necessary, not for the seller, but for the buyers, and as the buyers constitute by far the larger class, we must look for the greatest good to the greatest number. It prevents robbery, and every merchant would be a licensed robber of the people if he could, and if competition did not prevent him.

In regard to selling goods and what profit a dealer should be allowed to make, or be entitled to, there is no established rule or uniformity of practice. Every man is a law unto himself, and is governed solely by circumstances. His aim is to make all he can, and as quickly as he can, legitimately, of course. But this only means that he will sell at a 10 per cent. profit if he is forced to. Left to his own sense of right and justice, 100 or 300 per cent. would only be a fair remuneration for his time, employment of his capital, and sacrifice he is making for the accommodation of the public. What gas and sugar trusts and other monopolies aim to accomplish by their manipulations, is to remove competition. This done, and they have it in their power to exact any price and profit within the ability of the people to pay. Every dealer, retail or wholelsale, would constitute himself into a perpetual trust, if he could, and he does so when and wherever he has the field to himself.

Much can be said on the good and bad side of competition; the preponderance of the argument, however, rests on the side of its good offices in behalf of the many. But what concerns us here, chiefly, is its effect on our customer, and how far his chance for success is thereby lessened. As for improving his chances, that could hardly ever be possible, though in common parlance we say, competition is the life of trade. While this is so, it does not mean that competition enables you to charge more profit. Quite the reverse. It makes you give more goods and better service, and the public at large is the gainer by the stimulus that competition gives to trade, and the greater the competition is the nearer to cost will you be obliged to sell. The question, therefore, has much to do with the man or firm we have trusted, or are about to trust, with our goods. Without opposition, our debtor's chance of success could hardly be questioned, and the creditor, other things not being unfavorable, would be justified in considering the risk a good one. On the other hand, if in his locality the business is overdone, and the custom is hardly sufficient to warrant so many dealers, it then becomes a question, with the creditor, of comparative ability, financial and otherwise, of the applicant for credit.

It will appear, then, that a man's surroundings, and their bearing on his prospects, must be taken into consideration. For a new firm to start into business in opposition to old, established houses, is always, more or less, a hazardous undertaking; but the risk is not confined to the firm alone, since the creditors are always made participants in it, and this fact must be borne in mind. It is not an easy matter to establish a paying business in the face of old and well-known concerns; nor will the latter sit calmly by and let the new-comer get a foothold. His success will depend on his financial and general ability, as compared with that of his competitors.

We are made to feel reasonably secure, however, in a new firm that has bought out and succeeds an old-established stand. We know, in this case, that the trade is already built up, and that under a fairly good administration it will continue to run in the same groove. A new firm has to create confidence first before a line of customers can be depended on, but the successors to an old house start in with a lucrative patronage to begin with. They get the benefit of years of advertising and of acquaintance; in short, they start with a prestige that would otherwise take years to acquire.

All these points are of vital importance to him who is about to extend credit. The professional manager of credits gives them careful consideration. Every item of advantage and disadvantage that the applicant for credit presents must be carefully weighed, and if the balances do not show in his favor, it is not alone your privilege but your duty, as a good business-man, to decline the proffered favor.

PUNCTUALITY.

Punctuality is the essence of good business methods. It is the foundation wall on which great structures are built. It is the highway to success in life, whatever may be the occupation. Read over the lives of successful merchants, and of men in every department, and we shall find this trait invariably possessed by them and forcefully demonstrated. The man of business owes it not alone to others that he be punctual in his engagements and in the performance of his duties, but also to himself; he not alone puts others to inconvenience and loss by his lack of promptness, but he impairs his own chances of success. No great merchant, and we might say, no truly great man, was ever known to be without this quality of punctuality in a marked degree, and who did not practice and value it as a cardinal virtue.

In the matter with which we have to do, viz., credits, it is an all-important factor, and probably there is no other that exerts so great an influence on the affairs of commerce, in which we are all, directly or indirectly, interested. If every man doing business had in him the elements of promptness, of punctual observance of his promises, whether it be to pay a bill or fulfill a contract, much of our tribulation and distress, and most of our failures, would be avoided. The man who has an inherent sense and desire to be prompt, or who has made punctuality a maxim for himself in the conduct of his affairs, will make a halt when he finds that adherence to his principles is no longer possible. He rightly and prudentially concludes that the business had better be abandoned or reconstructed on a different basis. A. T. Stewart adopted the C. O. D. plan in his early career as a retail dry-goods merchant, as a result of lack of punctuality on the part of his customers. Having a note to pay one day, he depended, as we all do, and as a legitimate resource, on promises of those indebted to him. But these promises were not kept, and Mr. Stewart was obliged to sacrifice part of his stock to realize money in time to meet his note. He wisely concluded that where so much uncertainty and unreliability existed, it was necessary to adopt some other method of conducting his business, to avoid periodical distress—and he did. Every good business-man looks upon lack of punctuality in himself as synonymous with loss of personal integrity, and this governs equally in large and small matters. The man who is remiss in the minor transactions is not to be relied on in large ones, although policy and self-interest may prompt him to the punctual fulfillment of the latter.

The man who is not prompt can not be said to be strictly honest. If you sell a man goods on sixty days' time, you calculate on receiving payment at maturity of the account, and you have a right to expect and demand it. His failure to keep his promise is liable to cause your failure to keep yours. Being "behind time," is often as ruinous to the creditor as being made the victim of bare-faced fraud.

We respect the man, and we have a high appreciation of his business tact, who is always prompt in his dealings and his payments with us, and it is an appreciation which more should strive to merit. But a large number of people in business seem not to have any conception of this great requisite. They were born "behind time," presumably, and will always be "behind time," even in making their exit.

We all have on our books customers who have always been "slow pay," and who are not likely to ever mend their ways. It is a chronic disease with them, a congenital deformity, as doctors would say, but in ordinary parlance, "pure cussedness" is more to the point. The community seems to know their failing, and indulges them, very much to its own detriment and that of good business rules. It is fully as reprehensible to be lax in exacting promptitude as it is to be lax in its practice yourself. The large, representative houses have it in their power to do much educational work and to exert a potent influence on the business-men of the country in the direction of instilling good principles into their methods, by simply demanding and insisting on punctual compliance with terms and engagements. Some few of our larger firms have done more in this way, in educating the business public than have all other influences combined, and they rightfully pride themselves, and are entitled to credit, as educators and public benefactors. Discipline of this kind naturally results in mutual benefit, and in the private as well as the public good.

In making credits, the applicant's reputation for promptness should be carefully inquired into. Considerable latitude is permissible and is warrantable even by the most conservative houses. All other conditions being favorable, and we find the applicant is simply slow because "he is built that way," we need not refuse him. We can make him prompt with *us* if we set out to do it, and do it we should, by all means.

On the other hand, the applicant whose record shows unsatisfactory payments, and who has no established reputation either for "chronic slowness" or financial standing, must be closely scrutinized, and we must take the benefit of existing doubts ourselves.

In the case of customers already on our books, this may be said: We take for granted that the course of business is onward and upward—not backward. No man ever failed from the ordinary causes who did not give timely warning by hoisting the signal of distress long before the event. When a customer, therefore, who has always been punctual in his engagements, goes back on his good record, there is generally cause for alarm, and a prompt investigation is in order.

PRODUCTIVE OR NON-PRODUCTIVE.

By this is meant whether the principals of a business are themselves workers, and are earning their daily wages. If the proprietor be a hard-working man himself, and an equivalent is rendered to the business in services for money drawn for living expenses, the conditions may be regarded as favorable in this case. But if the reverse is true, and the proprietor figures that the business owes him a living without any equivalent being rendered by him, thus necessitating the employment of help and the paying of wages, then the conditions must be regarded as unfavorable. Few concerns can thrive under this latter method for reasons even outside of the wages paid, which the proprietor ought to earn himself. Take a small store, for instance, carried on by man and wife assisting each other, as we often find the case, and they uniformly succeed in their way. They both earn wages, and their combined earnings are more than their personal expenses. What would otherwise be paid out in salaries, and be a drain on the business, is made a source of accumulation to their capital. Husband and wife who thus work together, can safely be trusted, since we may rely on economical management and frugal habits. The ambition that prompts them in uniting their industry, also gives assurance of their eagerness to save and accumulate.

If a man has a trade at which he can work in conjunction with a merchandising business, his chances may be considered at a premium. As a matter of fact, a good tinner, starting a tinshop and hardware store combined, is a good risk if he only has a set of tools to commence with, and as a matter of course, has good character and habits. He can always earn good wages at the bench, and does not have to depend on the mercantile part of the business for his living expenses. The same holds good in any line where the proprietor works at his trade in such connection.

On the other hand, a man in business who neither earns wages as workman or as salesman, is out of pocket the wages he pays an employé for taking his place, and this single item, in the course of a few years, amounts to a considerable sum in itself. Nor is this all. The man who is industrious and keeps himself constantly employed in his business, necessarily keeps it in better running order. He also requires less for his personal wants than the man who takes his leisure; and again, by giving close attention to his business, fewer opportunities are afforded for squandering money in the various ways that beset the idle man. The difference in the personal expenditures between the two types of men will naturally be considerable, and the annual savings of the one over the other, added to his capital, will bring about a vast change in their relative financial conditions in the course of a few years.

The importance of these points is not always considered, but should be. The careful credit-man does not ignore them.

DOING BUSINESS AS AGENTS.

The class of persons we refer to are those who act as agents only in name, and not in fact. In it are included mainly such persons as have failed in business, and who have not been able to get a discharge or release from their indebtedness, which still hangs over them. To enable them to do business without the interference of old creditors, they resort to a legal technicality, and pretend to do it for someone else, and either use some other name, or their own as agent. This class is quite large. In many cases the business is done in the wife's name, the husband being nominally hired to manage it for her.

There are cases where this course is probably justifiable, all things considered, and where circumstances make it necessary, as a measure of self-protection; but these cases are rare, and the motives or reasons are easily ascertained. Generally the measure is resorted to to keep from creditors their honest belongings, and to keep property and earnings out of the law's reach. With these facts before us, which furnish us a record of the man's character, we start in forewarned, and our confidence is not likely to suffer abuse for the reason that we give it very charily. In many cases some friend or well-to-do relative is willing to help the man by allowing him to do business in his name, and representing him as his agent. The friend or relative in this instance assumes the sponsorship of the concern, and with his name also lends his property; that is to say, he makes himself responsible for the acts and debts of the agent. The agent's individual responsibility, character, etc., whatever these may be, concern us only indirectly. We are concerned entirely with the responsibility and integrity of the principal, who is usually a man of means and of trustworthy character. We may state it as a fact that losses are seldom sustained from this source, and the reasons are quite obvious. The help being extended out of friendship or kinship, and very often without expectation of sharing in the profits, the arrangement is one of friendly aid simply, and few men would so abuse the confidence of such friends as to involve them in losses on their account. It may be further assumed that the agent is placed under certain restrictions in the control of his business, so that the principal feels protected, and also that the agent confines his transactions within the limits of absolute safety.

In determining this class of credits, we act cautiously at the outset, because, so far as the agent is concerned, we should not extend credit at all, and in looking up the principal, we are naturally painstaking in our inquiries regarding his standing, and this precaution is apt to lead us to safe conclusions in regard to the extent of the applicant's claim to our confidence.

But there is another phase of this agency business, and one requiring much greater care on the part of the credit-man. It is where the man does business in his wife's name. In most cases, the man has failed, and fraudulently conveyed his property and assets to his wife. Practically, he has control of the property, and manages the business as before, using his wife's name as a figure-head only. The logical conclusion in regard to this stamp of individuals is that the acquisition of property by any means, and the comfort of their families, at all hazards, is the chief aim before them, and they do not scruple to attain these results, even at the loss of character and name. But what he has secured is only a nest-egg, and you will find him very cautious how he ventures any of his capital or property. He must do business to support the family, and in order to keep intact what he has; but he does a safe business, *per force*, as sellers are not eager to give accomodations.

Where the wife is the figure-head of a concern, for the reasons stated above, and where our safety as creditors depends on her, the nature of the risk must be considered apart from the ordinary way. She has property in her possession subject to execution, and we are safe so far as this goes, and our claims are covered by it. But in case of her failure, our chances would be worth nothing beyond what could be realized from property in sight. A judgment would be a dead letter against her, as she would never again enter the arena of business life. She would drop out and be lost to creditors for all time. With a man, on the other hand, under ordinarily favorable circumstances, the creditor is offered a future, and may reasonably calculate that a certain percentage of his bankrupt debtors will eventually be good for something. Experience proves that worthless claims of to-day against young and middle-aged men of average business capacity, have a prospective value, which can not be said of women under above circumstances.

Ordinary prudence will suggest our being cautious in extending them credit. We must keep considerably inside of the prescribed limit.

PARTNERSHIPS.

Many a good man has found out to his sorrow that partnerships are many-sided, and not all they might be. In union there is strength; but the union must exist in fact, as well as in name. A simple yoking together of two or more forces does not always have the desired effect, and in partnerships, the forces can never be measured beforehand in their relation to each other. It is always a matter of experiment first, and only experience and time can determine the wisdom or injudiciousness of a copartnership.

Union, or partnership, in this case, to fulfill its highest mission, must mean harmony, mutual confidence, and unity of interests and joint effort for a given purpose. Its very essence and vitality rest in concert of action, and, wanting in this, the combination must, of necessity, be a failure.

In a large enterprise, partnerships of two or more, when made for the purpose of combining capital and joining forces, each partner being qualified for a special task or department, are for the good of all concerned, and the great success of many of our large houses is due to fortunate partnership associations. I say fortunate, because whether partners are going to be congenial, and in every respect well-mated and of benefit to each other and the business, is always a matter that defies pre-judgment. Time alone can solve that problem. In smaller copartnerships the experiment is even more hazardous. There is greater reason for partners to clash. The work can not be divided so as to give to each a particular department to attend to, and one or both are liable to be dissatisfied, though notwithstanding their disagreements, they may continue together indefinitely. That this kind of an alliance can not accomplish what with perfert concert of action it would be capable of, is self-evident, and that there are a great many such, needs no affirmation.

There are always risks in forming partnerships. In selecting any two men, we could hardly hope to find both equally honest, equally competent, or equally energetic. Though truth will prevail and honesty is the best policy, nothing prevails as against an unscrupulous partner. The honest man stands no show in such an unequal union, as many good men have discovered.

Partnerships concern us here, however, in a more specific manner. In extending credit to partnership concerns, our attention should be directed to whether the association is a good one, all things considered, and whether the purpose for which partnerships should be formed has been fulfilled; also, whether all the parties are producers; i. e., workers, and earning wages, or whether they are simply consumers.

The next question of importance is to ascertain whether the business is sufficiently large to warrant the family and personal expenses of two or more partners. A great many of the smaller partnership-firms suffer too large and constant a drain on their earnings for family support, thus leaving no chance for accumulation of capital or enlargement of the business. Under these adverse circumstances, concerns can not get ahead, and more than that, it is evident that the ordinary vicissitudes in trade and temporary depressions are liable to cause both the firm's small capital and also the creditor's money to be eaten up while waiting for a turn. The earnings being consumed as fast as made during favorable periods, there is never a surplus fund to draw against. The establishment of a successful business demands constant accumulation of capital and facility for growth. The nature of business is to be progressive and aggressive. When firms stand still, it is because they *can't* do otherwise, for one reason or another, and this condition can not be considered a healthy one.

Every man, employer and employé alike, must earn what he draws, and give an equivalent for what the business pays him. A clerk is paid a salary which he is supposed to earn;

the employer must likewise earn what he draws, though he is not expected to draw all the business earns; in fact, his success in business demands that he draw as little as he can, so as to admit of the largest possible addition to his capital from year to year.

Forming a copartnership is one of the most important steps in a man's life. I am talking now of the honest, right-minded man. The scoundrel, who is ever ready to inveigle anybody and everybody into his spider's web, is never the one to suffer, even if he has anything at stake. The honest partner, to avoid compromising his honor and his name, is always the loser. Years of toil and accumulation of capital are sacrificed, and the sooner this is done and the association ended, the better, unless he is willing to be dragged to the level of the other. Make your selection advisedly, and not until you know thoroughly the man about to be your associate; do not enter hastily into a union. "Marry in haste, repent at leisure," is a trite old saying, and *apropos* in copartnerships. The antecedents of your associate-to-be must be without blemish. Not only that, but, if he is well-advanced in years, take note of whether he has been, thus far, successful or otherwise in his former undertakings. It may be said that because a man has been unfortunate or unsuccessful, this should not necessarily operate against him. The answer to this can best be given by quoting the advice of one of the shrewdest and most successful merchants of the last generation: "Avoid unfortunate men in your business affairs," or words to that effect. We may not believe in the doctrine of fatality in its application to business, but experience and observation have taught us that the advice is sound, and it follows that we should struggle to avoid the black mark, "An unfortunate man."

DOUBTFUL CREDITS.

Many cases, after the most careful scrutiny and consideration, will be of a nature to make a decision, pro or con, difficult to arrive at. If it were a question of making a cash loan in these cases, we should not be long in deciding, but the trouble is that we are prone to look at our merchandise as something that must be kept moving, and not as cash. In doubtful cases, consider your goods as cash, and decide accordingly. This will facilitate the process of arriving at a conclusion very quickly in most cases; for in no case would you willingly, probably, loan the parties the amount involved, even though the interest on the money should be equal to the profit on the goods. Another, more off-hand but business-like method by which to determine doubtful cases, is to take the benefit of the doubt ourselves, and keep our goods for better and safer customers. Whether this is the safest policy is susceptible of arithmetical demonstration: Take four doubtful orders, for instance, of $1,000 each. It is safe to estimate that one at least will prove a loss, and in these instances there will be very little salvage. Does it pay to sell $4,000 worth of goods with the certainty of losing $1,000, and the strong probability that you will lose even $2,000? It will surely be money in your pocket not to chance any of the four.

There is another dangerous feature in knowingly placing doubtful customers on our books. They may pay once or twice, and our fears of them are quieted; their orders are no longer so closely scanned; we look upon them as old customers, and our vigilance is set at rest. We often say to ourselves of this or that party: Well, he is good for this bill, and we will risk him for once and then drop out, but we do not always adhere to our good resolutions. The prudent business-man also takes into his calculations, in these cases, the condition of the country, and of trade. In prosperous times, he is disposed to take greater chances, and draw the line less sharply; but as depression sets in, either generally or at local points, he is the first to take alarm, and to reduce his outstandings to a basis of safety, and when the financial storm bursts, as it does periodically, he has little to fear from its effects.

Experience proves that in cases where the conditions and surroundings of the debtor appear in every way favorable and satisfactory, the losses are quite large enough without taking chances *knowingly*. How much or how little risk we are warranted in taking will naturally be governed by the per cent. of profit we expect to realize in a given transaction. On a basis of profit that would net us as merchants only 6 per cent. per annum on the capital invested, the credit system of the country would be restricted to less than one-quarter of its present volume. Mercantile credits would be placed more nearly on a footing with bank credits. To make 10, or 12, or 20 per cent. on our capital, however, offers temptation and inducement to take proportionate risks. "The larger the interest the poorer the security," is an old maxim well understood by money-lenders.

In conclusion, we may say of all doubtful applicants for credit, that our so-called Number One risks prove doubtful enough, and when we think we are perfectly safe, we not infrequently "get left." This being the experience of every business-man, let us confine our credit transactions to those whom we think are safe and reliable, and let the doubtful cases be served elsewhere. As a successful merchant and friend of the writer says: "There is plenty of good trade to be had, and I will have that, or none."

JOINT-STOCK AND COÖPERATIVE ASSOCIATIONS.

In the last fifteen years the legislative enactments of the different States have been such as to favor joint-stock companies for mercantile, manufacturing and industrial pursuits, and the benefits arising from such legislation can hardly be over-estimated. The law in most States favors and makes easy the organization of stock companies. It enables inventors, discoverers, and men experienced in certain branches, to promote their enterprises by enlisting many to contribute each a little of their surplus, and the investors or stockholders have, on the other hand, the assurance, by legal enactment, that their responsibility, legal and moral, is limited to the amount of their paid-up stock. To the investor this is all-important. His own legitimate business is not in the least impaired or jeopardized by the possible entanglement or liability that might arise from a partnership.

It is this feature, the non-liability of the individuals comprising a company, that we have to do with. Whatever capital is paid into a company, or agreed to be paid in, is all that the creditor has to look to, and when this is lost, there is neither moral or legal responsibility attaching to any one of the members of the company. There is, so to speak, no moral status, no individual integrity, back of it. In this respect, therefore, partnerships differ from corporations, each and all the members of the former being personally liable for all the debts until they are paid or liquidated in some manner.

We have become accustomed to corporations where the enterprise has been of a public character, like railroads, banking, and financial institutions, and very extensive manufacturing establishments, and the existence of this class of enterprises would have been impossible if the enormous capital required had to be contributed by a few persons. The whole country —in fact every money center in the world—is interested in public improvements, and the benefits arising from this aggregation of capital, all applied to one purpose, are unquestionable.

But when, as in late years, the stock-company plan has found adoption by all kinds of *enterprises*, with capital ranging from $1,000 upward, we are constrained to inquire into the purpose and motives of such organizations. To organize a stock company for carrying on a small mercantile business with $2,000 capital, more or less, can hardly find justification on the ground of any advantage to business in any sense. But that the promoters or managers have reasons, personal reasons, generally, which make such a course desirable or necessary, we need never question. These small "corporate bodies" are usually "close corporations," and the stock, and consequently the business, is all under the control of one man. This is about the only redeeming feature in them, in so far as it gives the business a managing head without any interference. It will be found that the manager, or proprietor in fact, is under a cloud; that prior business embarrassments, judgments, and claims against him, prevent his doing business in his own name, and the stock company furnishes a way for him to carry on his business without let or hindrance. In these cases the credit-man has only to consider the character of the manager, and he will have no difficulty in determining his or his company's claim to credit.

There is sometimes a bona-fide company, comprising a large number of small stockholders, organized for carrying on a small manufacturing or mercantile business, rarely mercantile, however. The promoter of these is generally the manager, but, as in larger organizations, he is subject to the dictum of the board of directors. Of these it may be said, that "too many cooks spoil the broth." There is no definite policy, and there is not enough individual interest, and both are necessary to insure success in any business. Usually, after the stockholders have wrangled over the affairs of the company for about a year, and the shoemaker and the candlestick-maker have had their say on the management of a fancy grocery store, for instance, the concern passes into other hands.

These are entitled to credit to the extent of their bank balances, and no more. No great harm is done to the business community by them. Stock companies have their advantages and their disadvantages, and the latter are rather greater than the former, in several important respects. For old, well-known firms to incorporate, has many advantages, and the credit of the house being established, only matters of convenience or of expediency need be considered by them. But in the case of enterprises that have still to gain the confidence of the community, the stock company labors under decided disadvantages over the copartnership in obtaining credit. Smith & Brown (copartnership) can get a credit at their bank for $10,000. The Smith & Brown Co., with the same capital, and doing the same amount of business, finds it difficult to obtain one-half as much accommodation in their capacity of stock company. Go to any bank and ask why the discrimination is made, and they will tell you that they prefer to deal with individuals, for obvious reasons, and the merchant or manufacturer, applied to for credit by them, will render the same verdict.

Credit is given to individuals, up to the limit of their probability to pay, character, experience, and reputation for honesty considered. Credit to stock companies is given to the extent of their paid-up capital. The former is bound to us during his life-time to pay his obligations; the latter, in case of failure, is "wiped out of existence," and with it all the creditors.

The granger movement, inaugurated in 1870, or thereabouts, affords a good illustration of coöperative associations and their outcome. Thousands of these were started. The grangers undertook to do the business of the country and monopolize trade by associating themselves into mercantile companies and appointing or electing men as managers. Too many men, too many minds, and the lack of experience withal, brought them to a halt. The old motto: "Shoemaker, stick to your last," conveyed a practical meaning to them which they had never before realized.

These associations were coöperative in name but not in fact. Like coöperative societies for mercantile or manufacturing purposes, other than so-called Grangers, they lacked unity of interest, and lack of effort in a given direction and for a specific purpose. Every business, small or large, must have a ruling spirit at the head of it to give its affairs intelligent direction, and this master-spirit must be in a position to be supreme ruler. Everyone holding an interest can not be "boss," and this is apt to be considered the special prerogative of every member of a coöperative company by reason of his supposed superior talent.

The lack of economy in stock companies is also a noticeable and a bad feature, and one that operates especially against newly-started enterprises. Our own money is one thing; the money of a corporation in which we have but a part interest, is quite another, with the ordinary man. That close calculation, attention to details, and saving of pennies, so necessary for new-beginners in any business venture, are, we may say, rarely found in stock companies. The average man, not doubting honesty or ability at all, would not make a safe bank president or railroad manager. There are really few men who have the faculty of administering other people's money as if it was their own. Of the trusted and tried manager of a bank, or other institution, in charge of the public's funds, it may be said, that he feels more concern for these than he does for his own. He attaches an additional responsibility to his guardianship over them which his own belongings do not, or would not, call for.

Bad failures of the stock, and especially of the coöperative, companies are rare. As they get but little accommodation, they do not become deeply involved, as a rule.

With reference to their claims to credit, *without an established record* they should be held closely to cash transactions.

WOMEN IN TRADE.

With the constantly-increasing number of women in mercantile occupations, engaging in nearly every branch of trade and filling all manner of offices and clerkships, excepting those where bodily toil is essential, we might reasonably infer, as a result of the experience and the knowledge of business methods acquired by them, that the number of women in trade, on their own account, would be increasing steadily and proportionately. In looking over the Trade Registers, however, we find this verified only in a small ratio. Why this is so, is susceptible of explanation; but we are concerned here with another question, namely, that of credit, and the claims of business-women to it and to our confidence.

Through force of circumstances we find women carrying on nearly all lines of trade, but those which to her are most congenial, and which she takes to from choice for a livelihood, are Millinery, Dry Goods, Bakery and Confectionery, Notions, Stationery, and business of the kind in which her own sex are largely her patrons, and for these branches she is not only well-fitted, but they belong to her by right of adaptation.

The business, then, in which we generally find her engaged, being thoroughly legitimate, safe, and free from any extra-hazardous features, it is next in order, in considering her claim as an applicant for credit, to take an inventory of her qualities of mind and heart in their relation to business—her characteristics, in short—and see how far they are in harmony with the principles laid down in the foregoing chapters.

An analysis of woman is, fortunately for the writer, outside the province of this treatise, which requires the enumeration of her many qualities only so far as they have any bearing on her case as a woman in trade.

First, we may say, she is cautious. This is an excellent quality for all business-people to possess. She is saving when she earns her own money. Good quality number two: In all her transactions she looks to absolute safety, and can seldom be induced to take any chances that might imperil her business or her future. She is eager for the dollar, but she is not over-ambitious, like man, and her conservatism keeps her inside of the danger line. She is not over sanguine, and to her a bird in the hand is worth a flock in the bush. She is afraid of entanglements and business complications, and is determined to avoid them. Men might follow her example with advantage in this respect. She is in mortal terror of lawyers, as she is of rats, and she steers clear of the meshes of the law by giving it no occasion for interference. In her perceptive faculties and intuitive knowledge of things, especially where her pecuniary interests are concerned, she stands admittedly as man's superior.

When we find her in business at all, she is there for the sole purpose of making her living, and she engages in no hap-hazard operations whereby she might lose her foothold. Loss of her little capital would be an irretrievable calamity, and she fully appreciates the hopelessness of her situation in case of failure. She is not devoid of ambition, but she does not permit it to lead her into trying to out-do her neighbors or to eclipse the world. She is simply content to make her living, and is not half as easily "gulled" by glittering schemes, as are men.

She is also a good credit manager, and if you can get her to trust you at all with any of her goods or chattels, you may deem yourself highly honored. She does not readily part with her property on a promise to pay, as is the case with many of our business-men. If she trusts at all, she wants good assurance of payment, as agreed, and nothing short of an almost absolute certainty will assure her. It need not be feared, therefore, that any considerable portion of her capital will be tied up or lost in bad debts.

There is another feature in favor of women in trade. They have no money-squandering habits. They neither smoke, drink, play billiards, or do any of the other countless things for which men spend, and feel they are called upon to spend, money, and the savings from this source, alone, will go far toward supporting a woman and keeping her business intact. In fact, in a small business, such as we usually find her engaged in, her chances, owing to her economy, would seem to be better than man's.

In the different branches of trade carried on, some stand higher in the credit-man's estimation than others. This is owing both to the nature of the business and the men, as a class, engaged in them. Of the houses, the nature of whose business brings them in contact with women, and who depend largely on her for patronage, it may be said that their losses from bad debts through their female customers, come within the average range. But this is saying a good deal in her favor when we consider that she does business on very meager capital, and her creditors trust almost entirely on her own recognizance in meeting her obligations. We might further add, that the financial status on which women receive credit, would not warrant us in giving credit to men, whatever their business might be. That she should be the recipient of such extra confidence and favors, can only be accounted for on the grounds of an established record she has made for herself in the mercantile world. We are governed by observation, experience, and precedents, in the matter of making credits, as in all else.

In summing up, then, and considering all her

good points and leading traits as an applicant for credit, the verdict would be in her favor, and our fullest confidence, within the limits of ordinary prudence, would seem to be justifiable.

CHATTEL MORTGAGES AND OTHER LIENS.

Not infrequently we find, in looking up the standing of a firm, that its stock of merchandise and personal property is covered by chattel mortgages, or that some dealer, who is already on our books, gives a chattel mortgage. Ordinarily that is equivalent to insolvency, and eventual failure, and credit is not warrantable under such circumstances, as a rule. Every dollar's worth of your goods simply goes to "the other fellow's" security, and surely your interest does not lie in that direction.

The law in regard to chattel mortgages differs materially in different States. In some it has been decided that the instrument is not good on a stock of merchandise that is constantly changing its identity; but even here, possession is "nine points of the law," and when the mortgagee once gets possession by virtue of his mortgage, it means time and expense on the part of the unsecured creditors to dislodge him.

Of late years the mercantile agencies have been very diligent in watching and notifying their patrons of all matters of record, so far as they concern people in trade, and who are, presumably, buying on credit. It is, therefore, almost equivalent to a confession of bankruptcy for a dealer to have a chattel mortgage recorded against him, inasmuch as the whole business community, far and near, will at once be advised of the fact, and cause every creditor to become clamorous for an immediate settlement of his claim, and the man who has found it necessary to chattel-mortgage his stock is never in condition to stand a "run."

Where fraud is contemplated, the chattel mortgage offers the readiest means for carrying out the purpose without let or hindrance.

It is not asserted that the unsecured creditor always loses his claim where a chattel mortgage is on record. There are extenuating circumstances, sometimes, but these, as well as the parties themselves, must be thoroughly known. It must be borne in mind that in these cases you are trusting, not alone to the man's honor, but also to the good-will and friendly feeling of the mortgagee toward his and your debtor. All chattel mortgages are so drawn that the mortgagee can foreclose at any time, notwithstanding the instrument may be drawn payable at a given period.

Not over wide-awake dealers chattel-mortgage their property, sometimes to relieve them of temporary embarrassment, without apprehending the effect it will have on their credit and the minds of their creditors. Many of them are probably not aware that every item of record is at once reported to their creditors, but such is the fact.

In the case where judgments are on record against parties, no one would deem it safe to extend credit, and yet a chattel mortgage is not only equal to a confession of judgment, but it makes a voluntary transfer of the property under it, to have and to be held by the mortgagee until certain conditions are complied with. On the other hand, the judgment can only be satisfied by execution and levy on property found. The chattel mortgage is already satisfied, and execution and levy are unnecessary. Attention is called to this for the reason that in the minds of many, a judgment is a more serious affair than a chattel mortgage, and that their interests are more endangered by the former, which is entirely erroneous. This may be said, however: While the judgment creditor is constantly on the watch for property to satisfy his claims, and the debtor's business is in constant jeopardy, with the holder of a mortgage amicable arrangements and terms have usually been made by which the debtor can prosecute his business without fear of molestation, so long as the conditions of the instrument are carried out.

To extend credit under circumstances so manifestly hazardous would be akin to inviting a loss and throwing away your property of your own free-will and accord, and this is assuredly not your intent, as a business-man. Astonishing as it seems, however, no concern is ever so unworthy as not to be able to get credit somewhere. The least that can be said of houses that cater to this class of risks, is, that they themselves are lacking in the elements necessary to permanent success.

The good, sound, conservative merchant has no use for the chattel-mortgaged dealer, unless the mortgage runs to himself.

INSURANCE.

No merchant should be entitled to credit who does not keep his stock and other personal property fully covered by insurance. In some localities insurance is very high, but where it is so the risk is proportionately great, and if the risk is extra hazardous to the insurance companies, why should it not be considered equally so by the owner of the property? Even if the owner be out of debt, and the loss, in case of fire, falls entirely upon him, it is still a transgression of good business principles not to be insured.

The good business-man has for his motto that what is worth possessing is worth insuring, and the expense should be regarded in the same light as any other current expense, such as heat, light, etc.

The case before us is that of a merchant who owes for a large portion or for all of his stock, and in justice to his creditors he should be fully insured; in fact, be insured for their benefit directly. It is a safeguard, and one which every creditor has a moral right to exact of his debtors.

Railway corporations do not, as a rule, insure. Neither do some of our wealthy real-estate owners. Their course, however, is justifiable from a different stand-point from that which pertains to the merchant or manufacturer. Their property is scattered over a vast area, and no single fire would cause them any considerable loss. But with the merchant it is different. All his stock in trade, representing his capital, and often that of others, is located at one point, and a fire means financial ruin, to avert which the prudent man is careful to be insured, the protection thus offered being more than an equivalent for the expense incurred.

Insurance statistics to the general reader have no particular significance. They deal with a large array of figures of losses paid and risks written, which convey no special meaning to the uninitiated.

To arrive at plain facts, we take the statistics of 1887, in which year we find the fire-risks written to have been $10,500,000,000 in round numbers. The premiums received for these risks was $95,000,000. The losses paid were $52,000,000. This gives an average of nine-tenths of 1 per cent. of premiums paid; that is, 90 cents on every $100 worth of insurance. But in arriving at this average, we include farm buildings, improvements, and also A1 building risks in cities, which will raise the percentage on mercantile and manufacturing risks very considerably, and it is these that we are concerned with; so that it is safe to say that one merchant or manufacturer out of every three, in the course of his business life-time, suffers loss by fire. And when the chances of such a catastrophe are narrowed down to one in three, not much margin is allowed. From personal observation, and in the absence of any statistics, I will say, that in the course of thirty years, one of every two dealers has suffered loss by fire; and this view finds corroboration in the minds of many experienced men. Of course, the risk is greater in some branches of business than in others. Of the printing establishments, for instance, it is safe to say that their exemption from fire does not exceed twenty years, so that of one hundred concerns in existence to-day, in twenty years not one will have escaped. Many lines of manufacture are equally and even more hazardous.

On a basis of premiums received by insurance companies for risks written, and judging also from long observation by parties in a position to know, we may assume, in regard to the ordinary manufacturing and mercantile business, that every man engaged in these pursuits for a life-time suffers damage by fire to a greater or less extent at some period; and even in the more fortunate cases, the total cost of keeping always insured bears no relative proportion to the loss.

Instances are not wanting where men have constituted themselves into insurance companies, and become their own insurers, on the hypothesis that what they save in premiums will cover an eventual, though never-expected, loss. The wisdom of this policy can not be reconciled with the facts before us, and it must be put down as penny wise and pound foolish, and in the long run, disastrous.

From the stand-point of the creditor, it is every man's duty to insure. The moral obligation exists, but there should also be a legal obligation. We can not coerce our debtors to insure, but we can refuse to trust them, and this will bring about a voluntary compliance. No man is entitled to credit whose concern and feeling of responsibility is lacking to such a degree as to willfully jeopardize his creditors' safety.

MISCELLANEOUS INFORMATION PERTAINING TO CREDITS.

The merchant or salesman of large experience will be governed in making credits by some things quite insignificant in themselves.

(1) In this day of traveling agents, no merchant need go out of his store from one year's end to the other to buy goods; he can buy all and more than he wants, and generally do it better and cheaper from agents than by going into the market himself. This does not apply equally to all lines of business, for in some, the matter of selection of goods and styles makes a personal visit imperative. The force of this argument is intended to show that people do not have to go out of their way to buy, and it is not natural for them to do so. When, therefore, an order is received from a stranger for a staple line of goods that can be bought in any jobbing town, and when that order comes from a locality not at all tributary to your city, but by reason of transportation facilities, belongs to another town, the natural and rightful inference is, that the man has exhausted his credit nearer home, and therefore seeks new connections. But even did geographical barriers and reasons not exist, it would still be wise to look with caution on unsolicited orders from strangers. Of course,

we all get more or less mail-order trade, and this can not be too highly valued. It is an indication of the buyer's confidence in us, which thus finds expression in his preference for us.

(2) There are houses who do not employ agents, and who do a large business, notwithstanding. They are generally old, well-known houses, however. They advertise largely by means of prices-current and circulars, and undoubtedly have inducements to offer, but, all things being equal, it can not be denied that personal solicitation is the most effective, and that, on an even footing, personal suasion will have the advantage.

Preference in trade is traceable to satisfactory past relations, and the result is confidence. On this hypothesis, houses become firmly established, as we say, and command trade, both through their representatives and otherwise. People do not "switch off" from one house to another without reason, and the reasons are many; nor is the loss of a customer always to be regretted. But, accepting the facts as we find them, they prove that instead of having business thrust on us, we find that a continual scramble is necessary to get even our share. Logically, then, when orders are tendered us without special solicitation on our part, and without any claims on the sender, by reason of acquaintance and previous business relations, close scrutiny is always advisable. We must, of course, use judgment in the matter. If you are handling a specialty, which you control, and no one else sells, people have to patronize you with or without solicitation.

(3) A buyer who is not particular about prices, though sure to want the longest time, is likewise a subject for distrust. In these times of active competition, no dealer can afford to be overstocked or pay too much for his goods. Recklessness in buying, both as to quantity and prices, does not portend success, and, as creditors, we are interested in every customer's success.

(4) We like to deal with the liberal "live-and-let-live" buyer. It is a pleasure to do business with him. This includes, also, the man who knows his business thoroughly. He knows what goods he needs and can sell, and he is posted on their values, and is willing to give value for them. He does not haggle; he either takes or leaves them. This represents the better class of merchants. Not quite so agreeable is the over-particular, cranky individual.

We find engaged in trade, as in other occupations, a liberal sprinkling of so-called "cranks," or kickers, but the mercantile representative of this class has the best chance for unretarded growth. The business community being, as a rule, accommodating and eager to please, our crank finds it easy to ply his vocation, and impose on our good-nature. He is forever being smoothed over only to find him breaking out in new spots. In his way, he is a perfect autocrat. Things must be to suit his notion, and reason or logic he has no use for.

Business-houses, and their salesmen in particular, are not long in finding him out, and after he is once "stamped and labeled," we know about how to handle him, and save ourselves much annoyance. He is labeled all the way through, from the office to the shipping-room. Opposite his name on the ledger is marked "crank." Except by special request no "monthly statement" must be mailed to him. The chances are that he has a special grudge against statements, and we are generally made aware of this peculiarity of his after the first round. His orders we mark "crank," when we send them to the shippers. This is done to insure extraordinary care in filling them to the letter. Change of quantities or the ordinary substitutions are not permissible in his case. To ship him quarter of a dozen rather than break a package for a sixth of a dozen only, as ordered, or to substitute even a better article than the one mentioned, are liberties which will cost you return freight charges, and entitle you to a liberal round of abuse besides. Even should the label on a bottle be pasted on carelessly, and be a little lop-sided and out of true, his watchful eye is sure to detect the blemish. He seems to live for and to have a special aptitude in the direction of finding fault with things. Nor is he ever satisfied to accept your prices and terms without considerable haggling.

But, though he is a disagreeable customer to deal with, the crank is not without some redeeming characteristics. He seldom asks favors; he can be depended on to meet his engagements, and usually we find him taking advantage of all the cash discounts. He rarely fails from any of the ordinary causes, and if he can be handled, and his trade be made profitable to us, we may feel secure in his paying 100 cents on the dollar.

(5) A valuable hint, worth knowing, is in regard to the course pursued by different people to obtain credit. We are frequently called upon to write to parties, telling them that the information concerning their standing does not warrant opening an account. This we write only when we are satisfied that we do not wish to extend them credit. As long as we are in doubt we do not write in that forbidding strain; but where this is done, our letter will receive treatment of various kinds. The man who is able and willing to pay for what he buys, will not waste any words or stationery on you. He will simply buy his goods elsewhere; nor need you ever look for any more business from him. The man who is responsible need not beg for

goods; in fact, it is a hardship for him to keep from over-buying of the many houses eager to supply him. On the other hand, the man who answers your letter by making explanations and asseverations of his intention and ability to pay, without, however, giving facts or figures, this man, four times out of five, makes us regret a subsequent change of mind concerning him. No responsible man will take your refusal to trust him, with equanimity; it is a thrust against his integrity. If he says anything at all, and is a polite man, he will simply tell you to keep your goods.

Experience has taught this lesson, that when we find men begging to patronize us, in spite of ourselves, their credit is at a low ebb in other directions. No man will allow himself to be snubbed if he is independent of us, and the fact that he does so, is *a priori* evidence of weakness, morally and financially, particularly the latter.

OLD CUSTOMERS.

To avoid losses from this source seems next to impossible. We feel that a customer who has traded with us for years, and who has always kept a satisfactory account, is entitled to accommodation of extra time, should he desire it, and we are glad, usually, not that he wants a little indulgence, but that we can be of service to him. No doubt enters our minds as to his financial soundness; we accept as bona fide the reason he gives us for asking the favor, and probably he is thoroughly honest in believing that all he needs is a temporary extension. Most men never fully realize their condition until they are hopelessly bankrupt, and until they reach this point, and can go no farther, they live in hopes of extricating themselves, and feel certain that they could do so if their creditors would only extend their accommodation a little longer. In many cases it will be found that "dry-rot," like some insidious disease, has done its slow, but very effective, work.

In the case of our old, and heretofore prompt customer, quite unbeknown to us he has gradually been running behind, and, instead of a temporary inability to pay, he is practically insolvent when he asks for an extension. Some day we learn of his assignment, to our very great surprise, for nothing is more remote from our thoughts than that he should ever fail. We console ourselves, if we are only moderately interested, with the reflection that he might have been our debtor to a much larger sum, if he had chosen.

Gradual growth and accumulation of capital are indispensably necessary to, and show indications of, a healthy business. Some years may show less gain than others, but a "standstill" is not a sign of prosperity. Every business man should be a little better off financially at the end of each year, and when we find a customer who has to sacrifice a well-earned reputation for punctuality and good business methods, which it has taken him years to establish, and of which he has just reason to be proud, we may infer that his course is directed by necessity, and that his future is not propitious. Of this fact he always gives us due notice.

The only method to pursue is to look up the standing of our customers at least once a year. The man who was in good circumstances a year ago may have lost money in one way or another, and have become, possibly, insolvent during even this short space of time. It is not safe to trust *any man*, year in and year out, without "looking him up" at stated intervals. This is not meant to involve the expense of a mercantile report, but simply the labor of referring to the rating in the agency books. Where these have remained unchanged, or have not been changed for the worse, from one period to another, we need go to no further expense; but in those cases where we find ratings impaired or suspended, it will be necessary to get all the new and latest imformation we can. We are often surprised, after a concern has failed, to find that it had no rating for some time previous. Had we been governed by a system of periodical investigation, we should have discovered this change in time, possibly, and taken warning.

Another group of customers needs mention here, concerning which it is difficult to govern our conduct by any fixed rules. These are the customers on our books who have never been particularly prompt. They are afflicted with a chronic "slowness," which never changes, except for the worse, and even improvement in their financial condition does not incline them to change their practices. Whatever their circumstances may be, they meet their obligations only on the most *earnest* solicitation; but for all that, they are clever men to do business with, and are responsible, on an average. Manifestly, the fault lies as much with the too-indulgent creditor as with the debtor; for, if need be, they can usually be brought to time by a positive demand. Although there are enough of these "slow coaches" to make a large class, we can not treat them as a body, but must do so individually and from a stand-point of the known peculiarities and condition of each individual, and our past experience with him.

It might seem that the losses incurred would be greater from opening new accounts than from those already on our books, but this is not so, with conservative houses, at least. We rarely "get left" on a first bill. The new applicant for credit is "sifted" thoroughly, and before an account is opened with him, his standing and responsibility must be above suspicion. Not infrequently we feel justified in selling a first bill with the secret determination to stop there; but, the danger herein lies in the fact that we do not always adhere to our good resolutions. Prompt payment of the first bill leads to the second and a third credit, and so on, until our first impressions and fears are quite forgotten, or, at any rate, are overshadowed by a few satisfactory transactions. We are warranted, sometimes, in the absence of definitely satisfactory knowledge, in speculating on probabilities and taking our chances for sixty or ninety days on one bill, when we would not be willing or justified in giving a "line of credit."

One or two swallows do not make summer; neither do a few prompt payments entitle a man to credit out of proportion to his responsibility, or against unfavorable surroundings and antecedents, or yet undemonstrated ability and character.

LIMIT OF CREDIT.

The limit of credit in any given case must inevitably be governed by things outside the actual capital invested, as much, or nearly so, as by the capital itself. No two cases could be judged alike in this respect, though the capital might be the same in both. We should have to take into account all the surroundings and facts, as required by our analysis of men and things, and this procedure would necessarily give us more latitude in the one case than in the other, irrespective of pecuniary resources. It would seem, therefore, that to draw a line by which to govern our conduct in the ever-varying conditions which are presented to the credit-man, that the task would be not only an intricate one, but one next to impossible of solution.

But all things have a starting-point, and we will commence by stating two propositions:

First, we know that the man whose capital is sufficient to enable him to buy for cash, and who owns all his stock, accounts, etc., free of incumbrance, is safe. We incur no risk in selling to him. The man who owes nothing, can't fail.

Second, we know that the man whose liabilities are equal to his assets is not safe, and the point is reached here where the creditor's money is in jeopardy, although nominally represented by property of various kinds. A condition worse than this need not be entertained, even for argument's sake.

We establish, then, a middle-ground between the two propositions; namely, between absolute safety and the point where safety no longer exists. The first proposition needs no explanation or argument, and the credit-man's task is made easy. But how far may we with safety diverge from the cash basis? That we must keep inside the limit of the second proposition is also unquestioned. We have, to be sure, assets, consisting of stock, accounts, etc., aggregating in all $10,000, and we will say that these assets consist half of merchandise and half of accounts and bills receivable. The liabilities we will suppose to be of equal amount, $10,000. We are here supposing by no means an exceptional or aggravated case. There is quite a percentage of business carried on with no better status than that, and, as in this case, where absolutely no capital is visible. To the experienced credit-man the case is a hopeless one for both the debtor and the creditor, because that the business, sooner or later—and the sooner the better—must be closed up, is inevitable. Then, what would be our reasonable expectation? No sane man would expect the estate to pay dollar for dollar, surely. Even under favorable circumstances, and with a good business-man for assignee or receiver, the assets would not net the creditors over $6,500, or 65 per cent. of their claims, and this may be considered a liberal estimate under an assignment.

What, then, would have to be our limit of credit to keep within the bounds of safety? On the supposition, justified by experience, that the assets of a mercantile firm, in the event of foreclosure or assignee's sale, do not bring over 65 per cent., the limit of credit, to insure us dollar for dollar, must be fixed at 65 per cent. of the inventory value of the assets. In the case we have assumed, $10,000 assets would pay liabilities of $6,500, and this amount must be established as the limit, and in all cases this relative proportion should be maintained. The shrinkage of 35 per cent. represents the capital invested, but creditors are paid in full, and this is as it should be. The man who embarks in business is supposed to risk his capital, and not ours, in the enterprise, and in case of loss or failure, we, as prudent business-men, should look to it that there is sufficient margin represented by capital to provide for emergencies. The nature of the assets needs to be considered, of course, and the probable shrinkage estimated according to their value and convertibility when credits are made, as will be seen by reference to chapters on *Assets*.

A case such as we have cited above, where the liabilities are equal to the assets, is practically one of hopeless insolvency, and perhaps not once in a life-time do conditions of trade change in favor of the debtor so as to save him. The rapid increase in the value of goods during the war placed many insolvents on their feet again, but wars can not conveniently be invoked for the preservation of sinking concerns.

MERCANTILE REPORTS ANALYZED.

[No. 1.]

F. B. CRESSON, Stoves, Tin-Shop, and Cornices, Dakota.
(February 12, 1888.)

He was formerly clerk in this city, and was discharged. He afterward associated himself with one Sardell, and in May, 1887, they began business under the style of Sardell & Cresson, in the manufacture of iron cornices. The business was continued for a short while, when Sardell withdrew, and Cresson continued, under the style of City Galvanized Iron Works. In May, 1887, he was said to have no means, whatever, of his own, and his record as an employé was said to be poor. It was said, his salary of $20 a week was insufficient to maintain his tastes; that his extravagance ran to women, and that he was in debt here for such articles as jewelry, board, etc. He had a small plant in his business, with little or no stock, and what capital he had invested was said to have been borrowed from some lady friend. At home he was virtually unknown to the trade at large; his prospects were reported as poor, and he had no credit. At present he is said to be still single, about forty years of age, keeps a small store, does not credit much, has but a small capital and nothing above his exemptions; is regarded as honest in his dealings; might pay a small bill. To some of the trade who have asked him to make a statement of his worth, he will only say that he has all the backing needed to carry him through; that a party with $5,000 stands behind him, but he refuses to divulge his friend's name.

ANALYSIS AND REMARKS.

Under *Character, Habits, Ability, Economy*, this case can readily be disposed of. He has no capital or responsibility, and lacks all the elements necessary to insure success. His character, habits, and associations are bad. He has shown that he has not ability or application enough to fill a clerkship. He has no notion of economy. Not known by the trade at home. Buys goods elsewhere, and evidently is trusted by some. If goods have any value at all, they are worth more on our shelves than on the books, in this case.

[No. 2.]

G. A. FRANK & Co., Northern Wisconsin.
    Wholesale Grocers.
(June 10, 1887.)

This firm commenced business here three years ago, and is composed of G. A. Frank and L. A. J——. The former is a married man, about thirty-five years of age, who, we believe, failed once some time ago, but is spoken of in favorable terms. Just prior to entering in this business, was engaged in shipping fruits to towns in this region, and not understood to have any means of his own. His partner, J——, was an explorer, and understood to have a few thousand dollars. They started out with a stock of about $3,000, which they claimed was all paid for. They have been doing a large business from the start, and making some money, but their capital is rather inadequate for the trade they do, although there is no complaint regarding payments, and we understand they confine the bulk of their purchases to one house. About one year ago, a representative of a house called on them and received the following statement of their condition:

Stock, $10,000; outstandings, $6,000; cash, and in bank, $200; liabilities, about $9,000; on open accounts, about $500 past due, but not pressing, and $1,500 due the bank. J—— had homestead worth about $800. Merchandise sales for first six months of the year, $27,000, of which a little over one-fourth was cash.

This statement was considered a candid one, but showed that they credit quite freely for a house with so light active capital; but claimed to scrutinize closely. They are regarded strictly honest, and we understand they are given what little bank accommodations they need. They appear to have credit for the demands of their business, but it is probably reasonable to suppose that their account is allowed to run along. They do an immense business for their capital, which would be, nominally, $4,000 or $5,000, but thus far seem to be able to turn themselves without any apparent inconvenience. Are very fair business-men, steady and attentive, but it is advisable to use some caution in handling the account, as their business is crowding so rapidly that they are apt to overreach themselves.

Supplemental to this agency report, is that made by a traveling agent: F—— is a good salesman, and a pusher. His partner is a nonentity, except as to capital originally furnished. Doing too much credit business for means; however, in fair credit, and seem to get all the goods needed. Think them honest and well-intentioned toward everybody.

ANALYSIS AND REMARKS.

That this concern is being "carried" by some one, or several large creditors, is evident. If in case of any set-back or dull season these should become alarmed, security would be demanded and probably be given, in which event outside creditors will find little left to satisfy their claims. They are undoubtedly honest and possibly solvent to-day, should they wind up.

The limit of credit allowable on their reported condition simply, must be very small. It is not likely that they can continue the business on the present "broad gauge" very long. *Volume of Business in Proportion to Capital* will aid us in our decision. Trying to bore a two-inch hole with a gimlet is not a successful undertaking, usually, and theirs will be an exceptional case if they succeed. We are better off, most likely, to let those continue to supply them who have done it thus far.

[No. 3.]

B. C. ALLEN & Co. Jobbing Town, Ind.
Dry Goods.

(Full Report, dated October, 1881.)

A has been in business since 1845. Is now seventy-two years old. After the war, reputed worth $150,000 and in A1 credit. At this juncture A bought out the managing partner and took his son, who had just finished school, into partnership. From this on, the concern has been going down, mainly from poor management. The senior is not, and never was, a good business-man. At the beginning of the war A was heavily in debt, through former failures, and obliged to do business under "cover." Though penurious in business expenditures, family and personal expenses have averaged for years not less than $10,000 annually, and continue at about that rate. From

1871 to date, only one or two years have shown any profits, largely owing to general depression and decline, but more largely to poor management. They still do a large business, and show $110,000 surplus, but are slow pay, and collections occasionally put into lawyer's hands. They are not in A1 credit, but seem to get all the goods they need. Homestead mortgaged for $9,000, in 1880, to satisfy claim for borrowed money. Wife said to own some valuable real estate. Assets represented to consist of: Stock, $135,000; accounts and bills receivable, $95,000; equity in improvements on leased ground, $8,000; lands in various parts, represented at $9,000; interest in business carried on by another son, $18,000; total assets, $270,000. Liabilities: On open account, $93,000; due bank, $22,000; due for notes and acceptances (bills payable), $45,000. No instruments on record against them as a firm. A is said never to have applied himself closely to business, paying more attention to outside affairs. The son devotes much of his time to society matters. Business managed by employés.

ANALYSIS AND REMARKS.

This report was the result of a special investigation made by a representative of an Eastern house. A large line of credit being involved in negotiations then pending, a thorough examination of the affairs of A. & Co. seemed necessary, particularly since the prevailing impression among the trade did not favor them. On receipt of the report, negotiations were dropped, and in the light of subsequent events, the Eastern house certainly showed both wisdom and conservatism in its decision. In 1883, the assignee of A. & Co. made the following summarized statement:

ASSETS.

Nominal value of stock	$ 95,000
Nominal value of accounts and bills receivable	80,000
Nominal value of outside interests	20,000
	$195,000
Appraised market value of stock ......$ 55,000	
Collectible accounts and bills receivable..... 45,000	
Available outside interests, about.......... 5,000	
	$105,000

LIABILITIES.

Secured to bank and others	$ 30,000
Unsecured claims	95,000

There was realized $78,000. The dividend to unsecured creditors was 37 per cent.

Two years before the failure a surplus of $110,000 was claimed. How is this shrinkage accounted for? Lack of *ability*, *economy*, and personal *application* to business, were the causes of this concern's downfall. The item of personal expenses alone, in the face of a series of unprofitable years, would cause a serious drain on the capital. The difference between the nominal and actual value of the assets shows great incompetency. It was found that goods, regardless of present value, were always inventoried at cost, and that there was a large accumulation of old stock (see *Inventory Valuations*). Bad accounts and bills receivable were likewise kept on the books, instead of being charged up to profit and loss at the close of each year. The actual condition of affairs was more of a surprise to A. & Co. than it was to outsiders.

[No. 4.]

SMITH MERCANTILE Co., Lumber and Mining Region, Wisconsin.

(October 12, 1887.)

Mr. P. Q. Smith, treasurer and manager, says the company was incorporated June last, with an authorized capital of $10,000, all paid in. Represented by merchandise. He says the business per month would aggregate $18,000; have $5,000 insurance on stock, and succeeds P. Q. Smith. Expects to carry about $20,000 stock through the winter. Confine purchases to about five large houses. Keeps bank account with the First National Bank of Chicago and local bank. On July 26, 1887, they gave statement as follows:

ASSETS.

Cash value of stock in store	$ 9,000
Stock in transit	500
Book accounts—good	800
Cash on hand and in bank	600
Real estate	2,000
Total assets	$12,900

LIABILITIES.

Merchandise, open account, not due	$ 500
Surplus in business	$12,400

Smith says, further, that he considers his interest, outside of the company, worth $50,000, over all liabilities.

The company's books show he paid out, in about one month in August and September, $5,000 in checks on two banks, leaving but a very small balance at present time. He claims to have about $10,000 now, gives liabilities of about $2,000, and says outstandings are about the same. Many claims have been received against Smith individually, and some are in attorneys' hands, unpaid, with which nothing can apparently be done but to await his pleasure, and it is said that when he has the money he dislikes to pay a debt with it. The idea seems to be entertained that the fact of incorporation was for the purpose of limiting his liabilities, and to block the collection of existing debts.

ANALYSIS AND REMARKS.

Under *Stock Companies* and *Coöperative Associations* we will find all that governs this case. Smith formed this company as a means to do business, and to defraud his creditors. Statement of assets and liabilities and surplus would make a very good showing in an honest man's hands. The sum of the liabilities is out of proportion to the monthly sales claimed. In that locality the proportion of cash sales is very small. Eight hundred dollars accounts and bills receivable is also a misstatement, because they are known not to do a cash business. The goods probably go largely into his own mines, and these, it would appear, are not within reach of Smith's old creditors, nor would they be to those of his company.

Altogether, the concern is not worthy of credit; still it is known that they buy largely from two firms, but these probably have an "inside track." Those who can not get on the "inside" had better stay out altogether.

[No. 5.]

MEYER & THOMPSON,   Michigan.

General Store and Manufacturers Furniture.

(December 1, 1887.)

Firm is composed of N. O. Meyer and U. V. Thompson. Ages thirty-two and forty, and both married; and they have been in business for a number of years, and our report of July, 1886, which was the time of their last statement, is as follows:

"Mr. Meyer makes the following statement of assets and liabilities: Stock in store, $13,000; factory stock, $8,000; machinery and dry-kiln, $7,000; warehouse and store-building, $5,500; factory building, $4,000; ground, $8,000; store and lots, $800; outstandings, $6,000. Total, $52,300. Liabilities, for merchandise, $9,000 on current bills. For purpose of discounting bills the firm executed a mortgage on the ground, on which all the mill property and store-buildings stand, and including stock in store, for advances to the amount of $10,000, which the First National Bank, the mortgagee, agrees to carry for five years. Advances at this time, about $8,000. The realty was already subject to a mortgage of $7,000, making total liabilities of $21,500. Surplus, $31,517.46. Mr. "H." says he regards the firm worth $25,000 to $28,000. Discount part of their bills. Mr. Meyer thinks by reducing stock and collection of outstandings he hopes to reduce indebtedness to bank to $4,000 or $5,000, soon, and then try to get stock in store released, and, if necessary, give new one on property not now subject to mortgages. He states amount of advances from memory. Learn at bank that it exceeds $8,000, but not stated how much; is still less than $10,000. Their property is valuable, owned chiefly by Meyer, and they have a good clear margin over incumbrances, exemptions, and liabilities, of several thousand dollars, and it is believed will work out. Meyer is regarded as honest. His wife owns a homestead."

According to a report of June, 1887, they decline at this time to make a statement. They produced an inventory, however, which showed a net balance of $34,000. They owe $6,000 on building, on long time, and current liabilities were $15,000 in January. They say now their liabilities are considerably less, but their stock is correspondingly lighter. Under our latest date it is stated that (understand the mortgage now stands as $7,000, but the actual indebtedness which it is intended to secure, doubtless varies, from time to time) the real estate is mortgaged, as heretofore reported, but they have a large margin over incumbrances and other debts. Their stock would probably reach $20,000, or may go to $25,000. They pay all their debts promptly, do a large business, and make money, and do not seem troubled in getting all the accommodations wanted.

ANALYSIS AND REMARKS.

Personal Property, Chattel Mortgages, Real Estate. Under these heads we find the key to the solution of this case. While we are obliged for the opinion hazarded by the agency reporter, it is the facts he gives that are of the most importance to us. The concern stands well, but they have been very slow in meeting small bills, and large ones can hardly fare better. There is no danger of their failing as long as the bank is friendly toward them. Unsecured creditors to any considerable amount could not enforce collection, as the mortgagees would come in with their prior securities, and this operates as a protection to mortgagee and mortgagor as well. The personal property, consisting largely of machinery and manufacturing plant, represents only nominal value to us. The chattel mortgage of $10,000 would fully cover stock, machinery, etc., currently valued at $25,000. Real estate is not available, whatever the equities in it might represent on paper.

They are good for small lines of credit, and the amount would have to be determined by the profit, and whether a house was willing and able to carry them. On staple goods to the amount of $1,000 we should have better assurance of prompt payment than this report vouchsafes.

They are too well established and doing too good a business to fear any trouble except from extraordinary causes, and a claim less than $1,000 could be collected, or secured, probably, before they would allow enforcement of collection by law; but in the face of this favorable feature, even, they are not a desirable risk.

[No. 6.]

G. H. IVES, AGT., Iowa.

Groceries, etc.

(June 9, 1886.)

He has been in business here since March, 1882, as agent for his wife. Came here from Indiana, where he was of the firm of Ives & Co. Was not very well regarded there, and was not worth, when he left, much over $1,000, which belonged mostly to his wife. He wrote us in

February last as follows: "I have been here for four years; have done a good, prosperous business, and am making money. I had some trouble last winter regarding the payment of my bills, but it all wore off in a short time, and now somebody is trying to make me trouble again. A few years ago I failed in business through a bad partner, and lost all that I had. Since that time, however, I have paid over $3,000 of those debts, but they are not all paid yet. The money that I have in business is money that my wife got from home, and it rightfully belongs to her, and that is why I have agent attached to my name. I have about $3,000 in my business over my liabilities, and about $500 of my bills due; no chattel mortgage on my stock. Doing a good business, though always slow in winter, and money hard to collect."

As he states, all his property is in his wife's name, and he does all his business as agent. He carries a nice stock of groceries, does a good, careful business, and attends to it closely. It is difficult to estimate his total clear worth, but he is generally thought to be worth in the neighborhood of $3,000, clear. He is worth little or nothing in his own name, always hard up and slow, and not considered reliable for credit. From Indiana we learn that his transactions there were questionable, and is not regarded as strictly honest.

ANALYSIS AND REMARKS.

We shall be able to dispose of this case under the head of *Doing Business as Agents*, also *Antecedents and Honesty*.

We could not safely sell him in his own name if we had to trust to his honesty, and in his capacity as agent we are at his mercy just the same, except so far as his wife's actual responsibility may afford protection. It will be found, probably, that should it be undertaken to collect a claim of any magnitude, the wife's property would not be get-at-able. He has shown by his statement that he does not mean to have his wife's property used to make good business losses, or for the benefit of creditors.

Accepting that the statement made in regard to the capital be true, and also considering that he is doing a fair business, we might place the total limit of his credit at $1,000. He would have to resort to open fraud, almost, to evade payment of that sum. Nearly every concern would risk this man for a small bill, say $50 to $100, and no doubt if the sum-total of his liabilities could be kept within the proper limits, there would be no danger. But in the same manner that one concern is willing to risk a small amount, others are willing, and an indebtedness of several thousand can be run up. This view of the case would not warrant any credit at all from a conservative stand-point.

MERCANTILE REPORTS ANALYZED. 189

[No. 7.]

N. O. PLATT, Town of 3,000 inhabitants in Iowa.

Hardware and Tin-Shop.

Just starting in. Is a young man, twenty-six years of age; married. Clerked for the last six years for J. & J., in this town. Good character and steady habits. Well liked; regarded honest and reliable. Intends to carry stock of about $2,000. Claims to have saved $900 out of his salary, and this is corroborated by former employer. A stove house and a hardware house, he says, have offered to carry him for from $1,200 to $1,500. Prospects deemed fair. Not a practical tinner, but understands that branch well enough to run it. Wife is daughter of well-to-do farmer in the country.

ANALYSIS AND REMARKS.

All the requisites to a successful career are furnished here. The fact that two large houses are willing to give him a line of credit, as stated, is an indication that they think well of him from a personal stand-point. For any ordinary credit in keeping with his business, he is a good risk. Although his capital is small, he stakes all he has and enough to make him careful in his management. See *Capital*.

Having never managed business for himself, the creditor takes some risk in the direction of what his development may be. A man may possess excellent qualities of mind and heart as clerk, or under someone else, and yet not be able to make a success of his own business. In fact, cases of this kind are not rare. For men to be their own "bosses" is sometimes a dearly-bought privilege. Other conditions being favorable, however, we are justified in taking chances on this one element of doubt.

[No. 8.]

B. C. DAVIS.   Town of 10,000, Ohio.

Furniture, Notions, Cigars, etc.

(May, 1888.)

Just starting in business, and a stranger here. He makes the following statement: "Have been in the sewing-machine business for the past ten years and made some money, which I invested in real estate in the town I came from. Property consists of store-building and lot, worth $10,000. Mortgaged for $2,500. I am going to sell this property as soon as I can and use the money in the business. Have no other property except household goods. I intend carrying a stock of $1,500."

Was formerly located at M——, and under date of June 8, 1888, it was learned that he owns a store-building, but not worth nearly what he claims. His business was selling machines, and these were sold to him on commission. Not known to have any responsibility beyond his equity in real estate. Nothing known of his character in particular.

ANALYSIS AND REMARKS.

The only thing we have here to base credit on is a possible equity in *Real Estate*. We may dismiss this case off-hand. Let him first sell his property and be able to show a basis for credit. As the matter stands now, he has neither capital nor experience, and of his ability and character, no estimate can be formed.

[No. 9.]

V. W. YOUNG. General Store.

Town of 2,000 inhabitants, Illinois.

Commenced business recently. Age twenty-two; single. For several years brakeman on railroad. Previous to that he was in a store for a short time. He has no means of his own to speak of. Mrs. Y. is quite well-off, and the capital comes from this source. Calculates to carry small stock, from $1,500 to $1,800. He states that his mother will put in $2,000 for him as fast as the business warrants it. Is a sober, industrious boy, attentive to business, and family well regarded. His purchases so far amount to $1,200. Paid cash $800, balance bought on credit.

ANALYSIS AND REMARKS.

This is one of those cases which we find under *Capital;* also, *Experience, Business Education, Character*, and *Habits, Age, Ability, Competition*, etc. In fact, the risk is equally

great in every direction. There is absolutely
nothing to recommend him for credit. His
character and ability are undeveloped; experience, he has none. His application and devo-
tion to business, for one of his age, is no guarantee of success, as a rule. So far as capital is
concerned, the mother will advance it probably
as long as she sees the business is prosperous.
If not a success and there is danger of failure,
she will step in as a preferred creditor in some
way for the money advanced. The only way
to sell him, if he wants credit, is on his mother's
personal guarantee of payment, until such time
as he shall be able to show his capacity as a
manager and business-man, and also show
evidence of establishing himself on a good
footing.

[No. 10.]

A. Van Slow. Iowa.

Grocer.

(September, 1888.)

Mr. Van Slow states in November, 1887, that
he is also of the firm of A. Van Slow & Son, at
W——, where he has $4,000 invested, and says
that his stock here is worth $5,000, and that he
has $6,000 in good book accounts; also says his
dwelling is in his wife's name, and that he
owns a house and lot here worth $900, and has
lands in Michigan worth $5,000, and says that
$1,500 will cover all he owes. Some good local

authorities think the foregoing statement is substantially correct; speak well of Mr. Van Slow personally, and look upon him as a good business-man. Others say, however, that he has failed once or twice, and intimate that he has been assisted by bank here, and were also under the vague impression that he is responsible to the bank for a portion of what he has; for this, however, we are unable to find any reliable authorities, and from the best information obtainable, find that aside from being a little loose in business matters and somewhat inclined to spread out, that Mr. Van Slow is a fair manager. Good local authorities think him worth from $7,000 to $8,000, clear, and tell us that he has credit about home for his business wants, and that no complaints are made in relation to the manner of his payments. In a report of March, 1888, it is stated that he is doing about as usual. Think trade is pretty dull, and that he is indebted $4,000 or $5,000, but regarded perfectly good still. According to our latest reports, he has been running along about the same for the past year, and rather hard up; however, he is doing a good business and can learn of no collections against him this summer. He has been refused credit in some quarters, we learn, on account of slow payments, but others are willing to put up with his methods, so that he has no difficulty in getting all the goods he needs.

ANALYSIS AND REMARKS.

Every wholesale house in his line of business knows Mr. Van Slow and his methods. His reputation is fully established as being a slow customer. He is undoubtedly good for what he owes, or may owe in the future. Those who sell him will keep him within proper limits, so that his indebtedness will be kept inside the "danger line." Though considered good, his credit is not unlimited by even those with whom he deals.

Punctuality and *Old Customers* will cover his case. If we are blessed with a good stock of patience and can afford to give six months, on thirty or sixty-day goods, this man will do to sell to, and his patronage can be relied on as long, and to the extent that it may be desirable. He is not hard to please, is not a close buyer, and if the goods he buys afford profit enough to pay for time and collection charges, possibly we may sell him; but we must not get too many of his kind on our books.

So far as eventual payment is concerned, that can be enforced; but, even the law can not secure our money for us promptly. He will generally take advantage of the law's delay, which is from thirty to sixty days, and he can also take the benefit of the "stay-law," which gives him four months, additional time, and in some States twelve months. This compels him to secure the debt, but does not give us the use of the capital tied up.

In giving this man credit, it must be borne in mind that his account can not be "banked" on. If many such would be ruinous to the creditor, as will be conceded, it follows that even one of the class can not be of benefit, and, consequently we are better off without the "Van Slows."

[No. 11.]

ADAMS, BROWN & CO.,　　　　　　Colorado.
　　Hardware and Implements.
　　　　(May 12, 1888.)

The firm is composed of C. B. Adams, C. D. Brown, and D. E. Clark. The business has been established some four or five years, formerly as A. & B., later on, in 1885, changing to A., B. & Co., with A. E. Davis comprising the company. In February, 1888, we have A. and B. alone, who, in April, admitted Clark, and the style again changing as formerly. They are all married men, aged thirty, forty, and forty-five. They have maintained a very good credit formerly, but in the middle of 1887, they were financially embarrassed. In October, 1887, they write as follows, to our request for a statement: "We have been hard up on account of slow collections, and in one or two places have allowed drafts to be returned, and have written to the parties to explain matters. There is no cause for alarm, and parties that we have asked for extensions have readily granted the favor," and they expected to have better collections, and plenty to pay their debts. In February, A. was reported to have homestead property worth $7,000, and B. had homestead and lot, valued at $1,500, and also other property, consisting of one farm of 160 acres of land, also having invested in the business $25,000. Also, were carrying an average stock of $22,000. At this time they appeared in better financial state, and no complaints were heard regarding payments; also, keeping a bank account with three different banks. Under date of April 8, 1888, A. & B. write: "That they have recently admitted Clark to copartnership, which expires five years from date, and at this time claim a net capital in the business of $25,000." We learn that Clark is a man of good character and habits, and is reported to have put in the concern, in cash, $7,000, and is possessed of some outside means. Locally, the concern, at the present time, are considered as being in fair shape, and are deemed worthy of their moderate business requirements. Additional, June 15, 1888: Do quite a wholesale business with the smaller places. Brown traveling most of the time. Claim to be doing at the rate of $250,000 per annum. Liabilities not ascertainable. Handle some goods on commission. Hear of no complaints. Learn they are indebted to one bank $5,000.

ANALYSIS AND REMARKS.

There is no particular flaw to pick in this statement, except that it fails to give the most essential facts necessary to be known, viz.: the amount of liabilities and resources. It is known that those who have had dealings with them in the past, have had trouble and delay in collecting. Their reputation for punctuality is not good, and how far the new partner's money may help them is difficult to say. Eight thousand dollars to a wholesale house would not go far, especially when it is already embarrassed.

Their credit seems to be good with certain houses to the extent of from $6,000 to $8,000, but they are presumably in possession of facts which the report fails to give. On the report itself, $1,000 on sixty days would be a liberal credit for any house to make. The conservative house would keep considerably inside of that amount, or refuse altogether, without further facts and figures, which they decline to furnish. (The mere refusal, however, of parties to give statements, does not mean absolutely that they are "shaky," or can not make a satisfactory exhibit. Some refuse because they feel independent, and ask no favors, others because they are pig-headed). It is reasonable to suppose, obliged as they are to ask credit, that this concern would cheerfully make an exhibit. Their refusal leaves us to draw our own conclusions.

[No. 12.]

JOHN SMITH, Town of 3,000 inhabitants, near St. Louis, Mo.

Retail Grocer.

Commenced this business five years ago; firm was then Smith & Co., the "Co." being his father-in-law, a well-to-do farmer, who retired two years ago from the business. Under Smith & Co. the firm was regarded good, and enjoyed a first-class credit, although the habits of Smith were not good, and this, it is presumed, caused the father-in-law to drop out. He declines to give a statement. His stock is estimated at from $4,000 to $5,000. Does a large credit business with the farmers, and not considered a sharp collector. No estimate can be made of liabilities, which he says are for current bills only. Considered responsible for a moderate amount. Hear no complaints.

ANALYSIS AND REMARKS.

The above report was obtained by a Chicago firm to determine credit on mail order received. The responsibility of the party would seem to be sufficient for a moderate credit, but the question comes up: Why does he go out of his way to buy goods? He can buy the same goods as cheap in St. Louis, at a saving of time and freight, and that would, naturally, be the place for him to buy. Men do not go out of their way to pay more for goods, or place orders to their evident disadvantage, unsolicited in particular. This case clearly comes under the head of *Miscellaneous Information*. If the facts were known, as they probably are to those who have heretofore sold him, it would undoubtedly appear that Smith's credit is no longer good where he is best known. Our thorough system of working the trade by personal solicitation gives a "good dealer" hardly any chance or excuse for seeking new alliances by correspondence, especially on staple lines of goods. We may safely put it down that if this man's trade was worth having, it would be secured by those houses to whom it legitimately belongs.

CREDIT IMPLIES RISK.

After reading the foregoing reports, which we may regard as applications for credit, for such they are in fact, or after examining any number of others as they come before us in the regular course of business, the question of "whether to sell or not to sell," is indeed a puzzling one, very often. The doubts and misgivings of the man of no particular experience in determining such questions are so clearly portrayed in the following lines, *On Credit*, that I consider them entitled to a place right here:

> To sell or not to sell?
> That is the question.
> Whether it is better to send the goods
> And take the risk of doubtful payment,
> Or to make sure of what is in possession,
> And, by declining, hold them.
> To sell; to ship; perchance to lose—
> Aye, there's the rub!
> For when the goods are gone,
> What charm can win them back
> From slippery debtors?
> Will bills be paid when due?
> Or, will the time stretch out till crack of doom?
> What of assignments, what of relatives,
> What of uncles, aunts, and mothers-in-law,
> With claims for borrowed money?
> What of exemptions, bills of sale, and the compromise
> That coolly offers a shilling a pound;
> And of lawyers' fees
> That eat up even this poor pittance?

> Yet sell we must,
> And some we'll trust.
> We seek the just,
> For wealth we lust;
> By some we're cust;
> And stocks will rust;
> But we skip the wust,
> Or we'd surely bust.
> —*British and Colonial Printer and Stationer.*

The term credit implies that we have parted with something of value, and for which value is to be given at a future time. It is not convenient or even possible for the buyer of the property to give other value in exchange, on the spot, and so we resolve to take the chances on what time may do. What it *will* do, of that we can not be absolutely certain. There is, then, a degree of uncertainty which attaches to all credit transactions, some more and some less, and to determine these varying degrees of risk, ranging from apparently "no risk to all risk," is where the critical task comes in.

But we need not be without our bearings. The sailor, with his chart and compass, though in the middle of a tempestuous ocean, is not altogether "at sea." By making use of the aids at his command, and the experience of others before him, in locating the danger-spots, his risk is reduced to a minimum quantity.

INVENTORY VALUATIONS.

There are safe and unsafe methods of doing business, as there are right ways and wrong ways of doing things in general. We refer now to taking stock, or inventory. The difference of opinion as to the proper course to be adopted in this matter seems to be very trifling; but the diversity of practice is very great. Strange as it may seem that people should willfully deceive themselves, it is nevertheless a fact that self-deception is of every-day occurrence among business-men. There is a weakness in our human nature which shows itself in a desire to appear for more than we are, and this holds especially good in a financial sense. Nor is the desire restricted in its effect on others, simply, but it operates with equal force on our own minds. Very few men are willing to gauge their possessions by a cash standard. Even when this is ascertainable, they hope to realize more, and accordingly place a fictitous value on them, which the future may or may not bear out. No deception is so harmful as self-deception to the man of business in the matter of dollars and cents.

We come now to the question, what do we take an inventory for at stated intervals, as is the custom? First, *because we desire to know how much we are worth*. For a business-man, a knowledge of his condition is necessary in order that he may conduct his affairs intelligently and with safety. Secondly, *it is desirable to know whether the business, for a given period, has been profitable or otherwise.* The last inventory, compared with the previous one, will indicate this. To know whether a business has been successful or not for the previous twelve months is of the utmost importance. To continue a business that is unprofitable is not to our interest, therefore a knowledge of such fact would determine us either to retire from it or devise ways and means of remedying the evil.

But, what is our property worth? In a strict sense, it is worth what we can realize from it in money, whenever it may be desired to convert it. Money is the medium of exchange, and is our standard for measuring property of whatsoever description. This might mean a "forced sale" valuation, but that is not demanded by even the strictest rules of business practice. What can be realized from the property in the ordinary course of trade, or what it can be duplicated for, furnishes a fair and safe basis of its worth. A stock is worth what it would cost to replace. It may be worth more or less a month hence, but all subsequent variations in value enter into the following year's profit or loss account, or inventory.

The plan followed by conservative houses is

to appraise their stock, personal and all other property, at the lowest cash market value. Some are still more conservative, and give goods credit for cost only when that is below the market, and at market value only when that is below cost. The first plan is safe, but the second is safer, and as no injury is done to the owners or anyone else, it might commend itself. The aim should be to appraise our property in such a manner, that, if we should subsequently decide to retire from business, that we should realize the full limit of our calculations. How many do this?

So far as ascertaining the annual profits is concerned, it is immaterial how the inventory is figured, so long as a uniform system prevails from one year to another.

Where the greatest mistake is made, however, and where the greatest self-deception is practiced, is on old stock, goods out of date, broken assortments, and "odds and ends" generally, and unless great care is exercised, a large quantity of these will be on hand year after year. To take these at cost, as is not infrequently done, is unsafe and unbusiness-like. They have an auction-house or "job-lot" value, and the proper thing to do is to ascertain that before each inventory, by converting them into cash by auction or job-lot sale. Many old and reputable houses, after doing business for a life-time, and thinking themselves well-off, have found, on winding up, that they were comparatively poor, or altogether bankrupt, from no other cause than giving a lot of rubbish a fictitous value which a money standard would not warrant.

When property consists of a manufacturing plant, and is partly composed of machinery, tools, patterns, fixtures, etc., the following plan is largely adopted in regard to values: All the machinery, tools, etc., are charged to machinery account, at cost. Labor expended in putting them up, fitting and repairing, is charged into expense account directly. At the end of each year the machinery account is credited with a percentage—say 10 per cent.—for wear and tear and depreciation. If the business was closed out the first year or so, this method would not cover the depreciation, but in carrying it on permanently, we can see that in ten years the first year's investment would stand canceled on the books. Of course, even second-hand machines and tools have a value, and when this is reached, the discounting process is stopped. It is simply aimed to arrive at a fair valuation, and at which the property would be convertible.

But the property of a merchant or manufacturer most difficult to appraise at its actual value, consists of *Accounts* and *Bills Receivable*. There are few accounts that we can be absolutely sure of. Those which we look upon as the best, sometimes turn out a loss, and the more doubtful ones come in all right. In order not to be misled in our calculations of what is due us, and what will be paid, we may classify our accounts, etc., and treat each class separately, by a general average, such as our past experience indicates. We divide them into three classes, viz.:

(1) *Accounts and notes which have been found to be uncollectible after exhausting all the means at our command.* These should be charged up to profit and loss account and expunged from the ledger.

(2) *Accounts against estates in the hands of assignees and receivers.* These should be charged, in part, to profit and loss account. We may, with tolerable safety, depend on realizing one-third of these; the other two-thirds charge up. This is by no means an under-valuation.

(3) *Accounts past due, in the hands of attorneys for collection.* This refers to such, where the responsibility of the debtors has not yet been ascertained. They are past due, and the ordinary methods of securing payment have failed. They may or may not be collectible by law. Some of these can be collected in full, others in part, and others not at all, and it is impossible to tell which is which. Charge 50 per cent. of these to profit and loss and you will not be far out of the way. It is assumed here

INVENTORY VALUATIONS. 207

that all accounts are placed promptly in the lawyer's hands when not settled within a reasonable time after due. In class 3 only "live" accounts are contemplated.

For convenience, accounts under class 3 may be transferred to "Suspense Account," and 50 per cent. of the total be charged to profit and loss. This leaves us 50 per cent. of their face value to inventory. The same may be done with class 2, Profit and Loss Dr. to Suspense Account $66\frac{2}{3}$ per cent., leaving $33\frac{1}{3}$ per cent. to inventory as available assets.

Because accounts are charged up to profit and loss and balanced on our ledger, does not signify that we are to lose sight of them. A profit and loss ledger, independent of the regular books, is usually kept, and old claims are thus looked after. Some of these are resurrected occasionally by watching them and keeping track of the movements of our defunct debtors. An entry now and then on the credit side of profit and loss does not mar the looks of that account.

The bearing that this chapter has on "credits" will be apparent when it is considered that, as a rule, we rely almost entirely on the applicants for credit themselves for the estimates placed on their capital and resources. Whether the estimates and figures are made on a basis of actual value, or whether unsalable goods and worthless accounts make up the sum total, largely or in part, is beyond our means of ascertaining. But appreciating the fact that over-estimates are the rule, and fictitious valuations are not infrequent, more from lack of good business methods than from bad intentions, perhaps, the necessity becomes manifest of making allowance for a liberal, average shrinkage.

PAST-DUE ACCOUNTS.

Out of every ten accounts that are lost, it is safe to estimate that only one is lost before maturity. The other nine were still good at maturity, and if the proper effort had been made at the time to collect, they could have been saved in the majority of cases. The fact follows, then, that we make nine-tenths of our losses, approximately, by allowing accounts to run, either by voluntarily extending the time, or by suffering them to drag for one reason or another.

Usually, it is for reasons of so-called policy—policy in other respects; but in no direction will it be found to serve our interest or accomplish a desired purpose.

We are confronted with the fact, of course, that mercantile bills or open accounts are not looked upon like an obligation to a bank that must be paid on a certain day and by a certain hour; at any rate, comparatively few merchants, taking them all in all, have educated themselves up to this standard. Where we find one that has, we find five who have no idea of meeting even a note on the day it is due.

But accepting things as we find them in reference to accounts, until they have become due, they cause us no anxiety, nor, in fact, have we any claim, in law, against our customer until then. It is only when the account has matured that the critical time comes for the creditor, and, even then, not till some days have elapsed for the debtor to make his payment. On a note there is three days' grace, and it is either honored or dishonored; but on an open account no·fixed time governs the case. The debtor may take ten or twenty days' grace without our consent and without our feeling justified even in making a peremptory demand. This much extra time we give and have to give, almost unavoidably, before any anxiety or doubt is awakened in our minds as to the goodness of the claim. After that, a series of letters are written demanding settlement, and more time is consumed, resulting in this, that about thirty days are lost, after maturity of a bill, before the fact is ascertained whether non-payment is due to carelessness, lack of good business methods, unwillingness, or inability to pay; and which of these four reasons applies, is not always determinable even then.

By the bank-draft system adopted by most houses, this loss of time can be materially shortened. Accounts not paid within a couple of days after due are drawn for at sight. If not accepted on presentation or paid when due after acceptance, it is the bank's duty to return the draft at once. If the bank attends to its collection department promptly and on banking principles, we either have our money or the draft returned to us inside of ten days or less, and the loss of time is, therefore, small.*

Now, then, default of payment having been made and the usual methods having failed to bring payment, we are forced to these conclusions: Either our judgment was poor in making the credit in the first place, or the premises on which judgment was based were wrong, or we acted carelessly and without sufficient circumspection. We frequently trust men whose actual capital and financial status would not entitle them to credit. We do this very often on the strength of reported good business qualities, a past record for promptness, and other favorable conditions. But when the test comes and we find ourselves disappointed, the party then has forfeited *every* claim to credit and confidence. In cases of this kind, no time must be lost in securing claim. Although collection might not be enforcible by law for lack of tangible property, yet the debtor has a fair business, and he can not afford to allow his standing and his prospects to be injured, and so by pushing our claim energetically, the chances are in favor of getting our money.

In the majority of cases, we can not know why bills are not met. To ascertain this at once, is

---

*Note.—Where banks are called upon only occasionally to make collections for us, inclose postage for return of unpaid drafts. It is only right to do this, and the service will be more prompt.

of the utmost importance, and to this end the best and latest information should be obtained in order that we may decide quickly whether our claim would be jeopardized by the necessary delay in trying "moral suasion." Lawyers' services absorb our profits and cause expense, and we are eager, of course, to save the one and avoid the other; therefore, when we can satisfy ourselves, *beyond doubt*, that an account is collectible by law, we may, in these exceptional cases, defer legal action for a little time while making our best efforts to collect without legal process.

But these cases will be found rare. After diligent inquiry we are generally in doubt as to the real cause for non-payment; but whatever the reason may be, it is tantamount to the debtor's untrustworthiness thenceforth. Delay would be dangerous, and as the customer is no longer a desirable one, our only policy is that which our safety demands, viz., to enforce collection by law at once.

I have divided our delinquent debtors into three classes, viz.: Those of Insufficient Responsibility, Doubtful Responsibility, and Undoubted Responsibility. The first and second brook no delay, for it is better to lose our profits in fees to the lawyer and save the principal, than by delay to lose both. In the third class, delay not being attended with any apparent risk, we may try to save expense, and endeavor, by the ordinary tactics, to make our claim. Our course, with reference to this class, will naturally be dictated by policy, or by our own necessities; but this we must do: Have a time and a day set when payment will be made. Insist upon this, as you have a right to; and, secondly, insist upon punctual discharge of the promise. If this promise is again violated, disregard further excuses, however plausible, and get your money.

It may seem impracticable or impolitic to some to follow the rules laid down here. They are correct, however, not only in theory, but in practice, as many houses can testify from their own experience. The more and the nearer we can bring ourselves to work on certain rules and principles, and stick to them, keeping aloof from all personal influences and appeals to our sympathies—which in business shows only weakness, after all—the smaller will be our loss, and this is applicable, not alone to credits, but to business in general.

It is an established law that "we act in the line of least resistance." To make our own collections promptly, so as to be able to pay promptly, requires constant and timely expenditure of energy, and is, therefore, in the line of greatest resistance—just the opposite of our natural inclinations. It can not be denied that nearly all our customers would be "slower pay" than they are if we consented to the arrangement. In a great measure, therefore, we are responsible, as creditors, for the habits they fall into, and the responsibility involves more than a bad habit in them—it involves our capital and our welfare. As between two houses that could be named, having bills maturing on the same day with the same customers, it would not be difficult to say, if only one house could be paid on time, which would get the preference. It is a question very largely of the kind of impressions we make on those who are our debtors, as to the respect they entertain for our methods and the degree of effort they feel themselves called upon to make for us.

COLLECTIONS.

A synopsis of the laws of the different States pertaining to collections and insolvency, is easily obtained and digested. The statutory laws on assignments, receiverships, exemptions, mortgages, limitations, attachments, chattel mortgages, etc., with which the business-man is mainly concerned in the collection of his accounts, are much the same in all the States, and are largely copied from the old English Common Law. Arrest and imprisonment for ordinary debt is done away with, and while this may operate, in some instances, with too much leniency, and more than was contemplated, yet, in the main, it shows evidence of advancement, and is in keeping with our more modern conceptions of humanity and sympathy for the unfortunate.

In Germany, France, and other countries, rigorous methods are still enforced against bankrupts, and imprisonment for debt is not a rare occurrence. In England, though the laws as they stand are quite as severe, they are not as rigorously enforced. Imprisonment for debt must be admitted to be a relic of despotism, but it is gradually being expunged. Where commerce is least developed, the clause is most enforced, and where we find the highest development, it is least enforced.

To imprison the man who is in our debt, and who is unable to pay; to shut him up and deny him the opportunities of doing anything to help himself or us, does seem to be the most idiotic proceeding imaginable. Besides the inhumanity of the practice, it is so thoroughly opposed to our own interests, so thoroughly "uncommercial" for people engaged in commerce, that we wonder it survived as long as it has. An Indian, who was incarcerated in jail in Albany, in default of payment of a certain number of beaver-skins (then taken as currency), made the common-sense remark, which strikes home, "That the prison was a mighty bad place to catch beaver."

One or two centuries ago, the laws and statutes were looked upon as fixed stars, and therefore unchangeable. Every interest and act of man had to conform to the law as it existed. The view would seem to have been held that laws were made first, and that man came afterward and accepted them, just as he does Nature's laws.

But happily we have changed this. At the present time we make and repeal our laws, and adapt them to the progressive wants of man, and of society, with a view to promoting the welfare of the community, and by thus reversing the spirit of our laws, we have made a decided move onward and upward.

Our legislative and judicial departments perform their functions no longer arbitrarily, but with due reference to the manifold industries in which man is engaged. It is no longer a question of what does the law allow us to do, but what laws do we need, and that will best subserve our interests, either in protecting or developing.

In proof of what has been stated here, we may cite the Bankrupt law, which at three different periods in the country's history was put into force, and each time, after having given the relief sought, it was repealed, and both the enforcement and the repeal were equally wise and expedient. At each of these periods, the provisions of the Bankrupt law were invoked for the benefit of the debtor class, who, by severe panic and depression, had become hopelessly involved. The interests of commerce, its life and vitality, demanded relief for a large number of helpless, though otherwise active and useful, members of the business community. That this law did not operate, and never will, for the benefit of the creditor class, directly, has been fully demonstrated, nor has that ever been its purpose.

Efforts have been made, at various times since its repeal in 1878, to have a permanent Bankrupt law passed, but with no success. The defeat of the movement may be taken as indicative of an adverse sentiment among business-men. In ordinary times it can subserve no good end. Its administration, as experience proves, is not economical, but wasteful of the debtor's assets. Its operation is subversive of the creditor's interests, instead of being beneficial, and they are better protected, or rather, can protect themselves better, under the State Statutory law.

Practically, the debtor enjoys all the advantages under the State laws, that the Bankrupt law can confer. If the insolvent of to-day can show good cause why he should be discharged from his debts, after paying all that he can, he usually finds no difficulty in getting an honorable discharge. The man who is entitled to it (and this includes all except the downright thief), can safely depend on the acquiescence of his creditors in any reasonable proposition for settlement.

Under our State laws it is "first come, first served." The creditor who gets ahead with his claim takes the persimmons. The wide-awake merchant finds no fault with this arrangement. (The law of Minnesota undertakes to prevent preferences being given or obtained, but in other States no such provision is made.) Since the creditor's safety rests, then, on his vigilance, it behooves him to be on the alert. Good management of the collection department has its reward under our present system, which is not the case under a bankrupt law. Under this, from and after the time that insolvency can be established by any act, all the creditors are supposed to have equal rights, and preferences or securities obtained subsequently are held to be unlawful.

Whether we are extending credit under our State laws, or the Bankrupt law, concerns the larger houses more particularly, and the latter operates especially against these. Many of the wholesale firms carry their customers for large amounts, in consideration of the latter's trade, and this arrangement is for mutual benefit. It ties the customer to some one house, and the relations between buyer and seller are of a very close and confidential nature. Whenever the creditor has reason to become uneasy, his claim is sufficiently large to demand security, and he usually gets it. The smaller creditors are left out "in the cold," in case of a foreclosure by the secured creditor. This happens every day. But under the Bankrupt law, the larger creditor could not secure himself, to the detriment of other creditors, and, knowing this, he would feel the need of greater conservatism in extending credit.

So, all in all, our State laws may be considered fully adequate to our business needs and protection, and the law of "the survival of the fittest" comes into play.

COLLECTIONS—METHODS EMPLOYED.

The large and constantly increasing number of collection agencies and lawyers, who make a specialty of collecting past-due accounts, would indicate that there is an immense field for work in this line. The best way is not to have to employ them; but since their employment by us is unavoidable, we must seek the best the market affords.

The plan of the collection agencies is to secure the addresses of attorneys in every town, county, and city, and your claim is sent to these attorneys by the agency to whose care it has been intrusted. The collection charges are usually guaranteed to be no more than if the claim was sent direct by you, and it is further guaranteed that claims coming through these will receive better attention. How far these promises are made good, depends largely on the agency, and much care is necessary in your selection. In the first place, their financial responsibility should be unquestioned; and, secondly, you should convince yourself that their selection of attorneys is made from the best ranks in the profession.

Lists of attorneys throughout the country are accessible to everybody, and it is no trick to start a collection agency; but it does seem to be quite a trick to get satisfactory service from most of them. But find one, *good* and *reliable*, and it will save you much time and annoyance in looking after your claims yourself, besides probably securing better results.

Where a good deal of collection business has to be done by houses, direct communication with attorneys has been found preferable. While this method involves more work and attention at your hands, it has the advantage of making all instructions direct instead of through an intermediary, and the attorneys will work for you just as cheaply and just as efficiently as for the agencies, if not better.

By becoming a subscriber to a good agency, it furnishes you a list of attorneys, both for collecting and reporting. The experience of every house proves that quite a large percentage of claims is lost by dilatoriness on the part of attorneys. This, however, is quite as much the fault of the client as of the attorney. If the attorney takes your claim and commences suit instanter, he is liable to be blamed and charged with an inordinate desire to make costs and fees, especially if he accomplishes nothing by it. In the absence of special instructions, therefore, he will always try to clear himself from any imputation of that kind.

When an account gets into such shape as to require the services of an attorney, the inference is that you have waited as long as you care to, and safety warrants. In either case you want payment of your claim. You have given all the time and indulgence that is deemed prudent or your own interest justifies. That being the case, let positive instructions accompany your claim, and these should be right to the point. "Collect, or if more time is asked, get security. If not paid or secured at once, commence suit and enforce collection by law with the least possible delay." Go on the plan that when you employ an attorney it is not to grant further indulgence or to accept further excuses, but to practice the law, and the more summarily this is done, the better for your claim, always.

We are prone to send our collections and depend on our attorneys for advice, and let them do as they think best. But the merchant needs no advice in the matter of an ordinary collection. He is his own best counselor on the merits of a past-due account. It is not a question of law, but of bringing the law to our aid and getting what belongs to us.

Positive instructions are of advantage, for other reasons. Attorneys are human, like other people; their feelings and sympathies are fully as susceptible. Acquaintance, and often friendship, between attorney and defendant, place him in an awkward position in matters left discretionary with him. He intends to do his duty by his client, but aims also to favor the defendant as much as possible, and the result is that valuable time is lost and your claim is often the worse for the delay. But whatever may be the relationship between attorney and defendant, if the attorney has positive instructions, of which fact he can convince the defendant, the latter can find no fault, for there is no room left for the use of discretionary power. Again, the attorney of your selection may also be retained by the other side. This not infrequently happens. Let the instructions include the request that if he can not, for any reason, attend to your claim as desired, to return it at once.

It is sometimes a question whether a claim is worth incurring further expense on. In a case of this kind your attorney may be able to advise you, and this will be necessary before you can give definite instructions as to the course you wish to pursue. We come too late with our claims sometimes, and where there is no prospect of making them, it would be useless to waste money. Such claims, by watching them, can frequently be made in whole or part, but if not, they can be put in judgment before they become outlawed, if the prospects later on warrant the expense.

SHARP COLLECTORS.

We are in business to make money, and not simply for the accommodation of the public. Upon this we all are agreed, as an abstract proposition, but how is it in practice? If anybody should intimate that you did business for accommodation, the accusation would be resented, no matter how charitably-inclined you might be, or how philanthropic it may sound. You would naturally say: "If I want to do charity work I can do it in an easier way. I can dole out my money and property without the work and worry of business." And yet how many merchants, and especially retailers, there are who conduct their business on that principle. To be sure, accommodation customers can be found in abundance, and goods need not become rusty or musty waiting for that class.

But that is not the way of the successful business-man. He looks sharp after his collections, and does not want customers who do not pay promptly. His goods will keep until he can exchange them for something beside uncertain accounts. He calculates that while he is in business he will have something to say about the terms of payment, etc. These he will make as long as the nature of the goods will warrant, but whoever buys them on his

SHARP COLLECTORS. 225

terms, is required to meet the payments promptly at maturity. Houses are prone to carry customers because they think them good. On the other hand, those that are not so good, or not good at all, have to be carried because immediate collection can not be enforced.

With the former class it is carrying voluntarily, and with the latter, it is compulsory, and, to sum up, they are carrying all their trade and furnishing them capital. This is doing business on the accommodation plan.

But it does not pay. There is neither profit, safety, nor common sense in this method of doing business. Even in cases where we have every reason to believe a customer responsible and undoubtedly good for his account to us, we are not justified in *carrying* him indefinitely, for the reason that any number of mishaps, beyond the control of any man, may happen, which will endanger our safety as creditors. Fire, floods, sickness, death, and innumerable other unexpected and unforeseen things may occur, and are daily occurring, which, though they may not always result in total loss of our account, are yet sufficient to tie up a portion of our working capital, and every time we extend an account, it must be borne in mind that we incur all these risks.

The largest and most successful houses are prompt in making their collections, and it may be claimed that this very feature in the conduct of their affairs has made them so eminently successful. The answer might be made that they can afford to be independent. Yes, and they always were, from a very small beginning. If business-men, as a rule, both wholesale and retail, would insist more on punctual compliance with terms and time engagements, it would be a blessing and a saving to creditor and debtor alike.

The timid creditor gains nothing by his timidity. Let your customer understand that when his account is due it must be paid, and he will pay it unless your judgment of him was wrong to start with; and when he wants goods and you have anything to offer him, he will buy of you more readily than of a house with whom he is already in arrears.

By letting accounts and customers run behind, the experience of old-established houses is, that you sell them fewer goods, in the long run, than by adopting the other course; but this is only one of the bad features of indulgence.

It is a positive fact that the prompt collectors are the most respected by the trade, and stand highest in the community, and another incontrovertible fact is, that they lose no trade by it that is worth having. A third very valuable point gained is, that you can handle your business and your capital to the utmost advantage, and give your customers better and more satisfactory service. This feature alone draws to you the better class of trade.

As between the easy, pay-when-you-like method and that of the house which insists on prompt payments, and fulfillment of engagements, it is not difficult to see and enumerate many advantages that the latter has over the former. To look sharp after our collections is one of the most essential things in business, and our success depends on it more than on any other single factor.

REFERENCES.

References, when given by strangers to obtain credit from us, should be taken with a good grain of allowance and be viewed with great caution. Much credit is given on the strength of these. Whenever any one refers you to another, that other's opinion will be a good one *invariably*. Do you suppose any one would give you a reference that would turn against him and be detrimental to him? It hardly looks reasonable.

The party referred to usually occupies one of several positions, and, we may say, his opinion is dominated by either friendliness, indifference, or self-interest. When not pecuniarily interested himself, he rarely knows the true position of the party seeking recommendation. Being under no pressure to investigate, he very likely looks upon the lenient and charitable side of the case and says all the good he can, for that is expected of him. He is called upon to tell the truth, and this he does; but he is not obliged to tell all he knows. We dislike to say anything derogatory of any man in trade, and especially if he refers to us and expects our good offices. Though ofttimes perversive of good, we may look upon this charitable phase of human nature in business as very exalted and highly commendable of itself.

If, on the other hand, the referee, or party referred to, is interested pecuniarily in the referring party, who is a customer, we will say, though not perhaps, the most desirable in every way, the law of self-interest is apt to come to the surface. If good can be said, we say it with great pleasure and satisfaction. If not so good, we say less. Our own business relations and safety depend upon his success, and the latter, again, depends upon his ability to get accommodations from others, and our cognizance of this fact prompts us to aid him all we can. In all this, it may be said, the mind operates quite unconsciously of any wrong-doing.

Another feature is this: There is hardly a man who has not one or more friends, especially if he is a business-man. Some one of the many he trades with can always be relied on to give a good account of him, though so far as the many are concerned, this would probably have to pass for a "minority report." A man always puts his best foot forward, and in giving references, he will be sure to give such as will benefit him. An opinion from all those he deals with would probably differ, and furnish a more correct basis to work from.

Bank references are usually considered of a very high order, and place the giver very high in our estimation. The man who can lay claim to the right of referring to his banker, we look upon as gilt-edged. But we find by experience that a banker's opinion, as he gives it to us, at any rate, is very liable to be misleading. Indifference, or self-interest, also govern his statements. It is always with reluctance that bankers allow themselves to be used as informers or mercantile agencies. They studiously avoid saying anything of a disparaging nature of their townspeople, whether customers or not. That they usually know more than they tell, is unquestionable.

If the banker, whose opinion you ask of a certain merchant, happens to be a creditor himself, he will tell you that he has confidence enough in him to loan him money, and this he emphasizes in a manner so as to carry the conviction that this ought to be sufficient evidence of his worthiness and claim to credit. Our minds are set at rest by this practical demonstration of confidence, but in case the party fails soon after, what do we find? It is found that the banker *was* a creditor, possibly is a creditor still, but if so, he is, nine cases out of ten, a secured creditor, while you are not. The banker's confidence, after all, seems not to have been in the party so much as in his collaterals.

We find no fault with the banks for protecting themselves, and this is not brought against them as an arraignment. Every creditor would do the same. This is brought up merely to show that because a man is a borrower at a bank, is not necessarily a sure sign that he is a safe man for us to trust. The banker, in the first place, is a privileged character. The borrower is required to make a minute statement of his affairs, and he is prepared to give it if he desires a loan. In regard to such statements, the banker also enjoys superior facilities for having them corroborated and their correctness substantiated. On the other hand, the merchant who seeks to place his goods and secure a customer in a mercantile way, finds it more difficult to get statements; they are not so eagerly furnished; in fact, we are liable to offend by the mere asking for them.

Inquire of a banker regarding the standing of any business firm in his locality, and his answer will invariably be favorable; rarely unfavorable or damaging. Even if the house in question has been known to be slow in meeting its obligations —"well, that does not signify; everybody is a little slow, now." But ask the banker to discount the paper of this same concern, without recourse, though with a liberal commission, and it will be a rare exception when he is not out of funds just about that time.

This simply proves the position taken, that men in business like to say good things of each other, rather than the reverse. It seems to do us good, to give us exceeding pleasure, to be able to speak well of another, particularly when we can do so conscientiously and by reason of long acquaintance and from personal knowledge.

What has been stated above pertains to the references *ordinarily* given by one man to another, or by one house to another, and where simply opinions are dealt in without serious consideration, as is too often the case. Their value, however, can be greatly enhanced and made to perform the very best of offices, as, for instance, when a customer gives us as reference a reputable firm, and that firm, in turn, is willing to allow us access to the man's ledger account or give us a transcript of the transactions with him. This procedure furnishes us with valuable data, and with these we can form our own and intelligent conclusions. If the transactions cover a long period of years they will furnish particularly good evidence of the party's manner of doing business, and we can readily determine whether his account would be a desirable acquisition, or not; for what is satisfactory to one house is not always so to another. And if we are given several references, and are accorded similar privileges in each case, we then command information of a very superior and reliable nature. Instead of mere opinions, we are placed in possession of facts and figures and an established record, and references which enable us to obtain these details are invaluable to the credit-man.

The importance of this class of reference has received recognition at the hands of several leading lines of trade. In the Wholesale Clothing trade nearly all the large houses, East and West, have formed themselves into an association, the object of which is "mutual protection and assistance in the matter of credits." A committee is appointed, "clothed" with authority to ask of any of the members transcripts of accounts of any of their customers. Not only the past transactions of a dealer are thus made serviceable for our purpose, but his present liabilities to that particular branch of trade are ascertainable. A retail clothing merchant's sum-total of indebtedness to the trade is arrived at with exactness by this system, and if his liabilities exceed the justifiable "limit of credit," or, if he falls behind in his payments at any time, the fact can be at once known to every member of the association.

The same system prevails with the Jewelers and the Furniture trade; and their separate organizations, for mutual protection, have attained a high degree of usefulness. A bureau is created, and the information required by members is obtained by an actuary appointed by the bureau. To some extent other lines of trade make use of this method, also, but it is by no means adopted universally.

It will be seen that information received under these conditions is valuable; but to create the conditions first requires coöperation of business-houses. As a matter of fact, where this mutual understanding and coöperation exist, references cease to be of any great importance, since, with or without them, the standing of a new applicant for credit could, readily, and naturally would be looked up; nor would the inquiries be confined to the house specially referred to.

Agencies have been established and exist which work on this plan, but their usefulness is necessarily limited. Were the universal adoption of the plan by all houses feasible, however (which it is not, for obvious reasons), we might look for great benefits and greater safety to our interests as creditors. The present mercantile reports, giving us the character, ability, capital, etc., of buyers, in conjunction with reports from the sellers, giving us the total amount of liabilities of said buyers and their manner of meeting them, would place us in position to act very advisedly, and we might say, unerringly. What our debtors own is important for us to know, but what they owe is equally important, for a knowledge of the assets only, in itself, is not of any particular value. It is an exact knowledge of the *proportion* of assets to liabilities, in the case of our debtor, that must be arrived at.

There exists among the trade at large a commendable degree of courtesy. Not only in respect to honoring references, which, of course, it is a duty we owe our customer when he refers to us, but among houses, generally, we find a disposition to be of service to each other in giving information, even without the special privilege that a reference confers; and this fraternal feeling can not be developed too much.

That the practice of giving and taking references saves much time and perplexity in the ordinary course of business, is undeniable; but in our acceptance and use of them caution is enjoined the same as in accepting gold coins—we must carefully weigh and examine them.

COMMERCIAL TRAVELERS.

To sell, and very often to create a market for, the line of goods he represents, is the *forte* of the traveling agent; but this, though done successfully, may after all be fraught with disastrous consequences to the party furnishing the goods and capital. With energy and ability as salesman, it is of the utmost importance that he should combine with these another qualification, viz.: judgment in making credits. The old and experienced agent becomes, by constant practice and contact with business-people, a keen judge of human nature, of men's motives and honesty; but all have not reached that point, and some, having mistaken their calling, never will. Anybody can give away goods; that is, make sales without regard to cost or profit, or by selling to irresponsible parties, and plenty of these can always be found.

A very large proportion of the credits throughout the country are made directly by agents, or based on their opinions, and in a large measure the prosperity of most houses is in their hands. All shades of competency(?) are met with among traveling men on this head; the difference between them in the matter of giving credit being as great as it is in their various other capacities. Some agents start out with the idea that their sole business is to make sales, and that it is the firm's affair to determine the rest. Of course, the firm has the privilege of accepting or rejecting, but we can not afford to have men, under pay and expense, waste their time on parties whose orders have to be declined. That does not pay, and it further indicates a great lack of a vital something, when a representative shows such indifference to our interests. Coming in daily contact with the trade in his capacity, he is not only the representative of his firm, but he is at the moment the firm "de facto," and not until he realizes this, and that on his acts and judgment depends the welfare of his house, will he make himself a valuable man and indispensable co-worker. It is the commercial traveler in our day who transacts most of the business of selling and distributing, and the authority necessarily given allows him all the discretionary power and latitude, that his principals could wisely exercise themselves. And this is necessary, for to enable our representative to do the best for us, he must have our fullest confidence, and be allowed the utmost freedom in the use of his faculties; and to the great body of agents all this is given, with mutually advantageous results. Of course, only those are entitled to such confidential consideration whose past services have been marked by uniformly good judgment and business capabilities.

A eulogy of the traveling man is not contemplated, but that he forms the backbone and sinews of our commercial growth, and that to him is due, in a large measure, its rapid development, must be unhesitatingly admitted. This much is necessary to say of him, in a general way, and in order to arrive at a proper appreciation of his vocation, that on him devolves the executive part of nearly all our commercial transactions, and the implicit trust reposed in him is either for good or for harm to his firm, according as he is a co-worker, or not, in the fullest sense of that term. With respect to determining a buyer's claim to credit and our safety as creditors, the traveling agent has certainly every opportunity afforded him for exercising judgment. Coming in personal contact with the buyer, as he necessarily does, an estimate of his ability, character, habits, and "make-up" generally, is made possible to a practiced mind. Being where the business is carried on, he is also enabled to make observations of its management, the attention given to it, and whether, on the whole, the requirements necessary to success are fulfilled, or in some vital points overlooked or neglected. Every business carries to our minds impressions, and even convictions, of its condition, whether prosperous or otherwise, and our intuitive senses become wonderfully alert through constant use. The same holds good of men, and our first impressions of them. Being, furthermore, in the buyer's place of residence, the agent can obtain information of a general and often of a specific character from the neighbors and townspeople, all of which will aid him materially in forming his opinion.

All these facilities are at the command of the agent, and should be utilized by him, to the end that his recommendations may be judicious, or that the information given by him may be used to corroborate agency or other reports in possession of his principals.

To the man of long service on the road, advice is not proffered, but to the less experienced, or those naturally a little remiss in the matter of credits, as many of them are, a careful notice of the suggestions made in the preceding chapters will redound largely to their advantage, and be of immeasurable assistance to their respective firms.

One of the shortcomings of the average agent is, that he seldom gets *actual figures* as to a customer's standing, even when a special request is made to that effect. In lieu of a statement he will give it as his opinion that the party is all right, without, however, being able to give any specific grounds for his reasoning. His modesty and timidity in getting at facts are only equaled by the customer's incompetency or carelessness in keeping his books and affairs. In many instances we know the agent is unable to get a statement, for the reason that the proprietor himself can only make a rough guess at his condition, and as for details, classification of property, etc., he is quite at sea. With this class of merchants, if an inventory is ever taken, the books never show evidences of it; they never know their true condition from a monetary standard, and would be disheartened, very often, if they did know. But even in these cases the agent can gather something, if he perseveres in the right direction, and if he knows what points of information are of greatest importance to obtain.

It is a great satisfaction and relief to be able to feel that an agent's opinion can be relied on, and that his uniform good judgment warrants us in accepting his dictum in all cases, conflicting opinions to the contrary notwithstanding; nor can it be otherwise than gratifying to him to have won respect for his judgment to such an extent.

In conclusion, we would say, that every traveling man should aim to make his recommendations on credits unquestioned, and his opinions law, in the estimation of his principals.

PERSONAL INTERVIEWS VERSUS REPORTS.

We will undertake to show the comparative advantages and disadvantages of the two methods in determining credit. The time was when every merchant found it necessary to repair to the markets once a year, at least, to buy his spring or fall stock of goods. If he was a time customer, as nearly all were, say fifty years ago, he brought his cash with him to liquidate previous purchases, thus making his account good for another credit. There was personal contact and acquaintance between buyer and seller, but this no longer exists to any appreciable extent. The business of to-day is done mainly through traveling agents and by correspondence, so that no opportunity is afforded the merchant or credit-man of exercising his judgment of character and of men. Half a century ago the New York merchant prided himself on his keen, perceptive faculties in judging human nature. Constant practice undoubtedly made them adepts in this special vocation, and questions of credit were probably no more vexatious to them than they are to us. At any rate, they were always ready to back their opinions, if favorable, by risking their goods.

Did they ever lose? The losses sustained by

New York merchants, say from 1800 to 1850, were enormous, but they also reaped large profits, and neither the losses nor the long time, six to twelve months usually, prevented them from making fortunes.

Is a personal interview between a would-be debtor and creditor an advantage, or detriment, in determining credit? It may be either, according to circumstances. Both methods, personal interviews and reports, have their compensating features. The accomplished rogue impresses you favorably very often. He has made it his study to give good impressions, and he is as well up in his profession as the merchant—he is often the more expert of the two. Even though you have unfavorable reports of him, in his case forewarned is not forearmed always. He manages, not infrequently, to brush away any ill-favored comments that his neighbors or reporters may have made, or that in any way preceded him. A personal interview gives him that opportunity, and he, more than likely, is not only able to make a satisfactory explanation, but able to ingratiate himself into your confidence and get your sympathy as well. Per contra, when we have only reports to govern us, we have cold-blooded facts to deal with; at least we accept them as facts, and our cool reasoning faculties and judgment alone are exercised, and our sympathies are in no wise appealed to or endangered.

It is not to be denied that now and then men have been badly used and their reputation injured without just cause; but, after all, these cases are rare, and we may with safety conclude that when injurious reports are circulated, that there is some foundation for them, as a rule. Where there is smoke there is always some fire.

CHRONIC BORROWERS.

There is a class of individuals in all mercantile communities who may be likened to parasitic or fungus growths. Like the latter, they subsist on their neighbors. These parasites in business, or out of business, are always asking us for a loan till to-morrow or next day, and no sooner get one loan paid up than they are around for another.

There is a class of men in business who are always borrowing from Peter to pay Paul, and they get as many Peters on the string as the neighborhood and their circle of acquaintances will afford. They are thoroughly imbued with the idea that business is done for their especial accommodation, and accordingly press all their neighbors and acquaintances, however slight, into service, keeping at the same time close watch on each one's turn. The pressing obligation is always pressing, and seems never to be discharged; and probably it never is, being only shifted from one day to another, and from one shoulder to another. There is hardly a house that does not carry in its cash drawer several I. O. U.'s returnable to-morrow, and which represent to the cashier so much cash in balancing his accounts. At the end of the year more or less of these are always unredeemed and uncollectible. The most consoling thing about a loss of this kind is that when your customer suspends payments with you, he suspends his visits to you also, and in this there is some compensation at least.

But there is a more business-like way of getting at this. The man of business tact, belonging to this same class, however, has a more genteel way. He wouldn't do as the other fellow does; i. e , ask for a loan. That looks too much like borrowing. He runs in and asks you to exchange checks or notes with him. He knows whose checks are always good at the banks. You do not catch him exchanging his check for one that there is any question about; it must be gilt-edged to be fit for an exchange with his. His check, you know (but you do not always), will be all right to-morrow by the time it gets 'round to the clearing-house. Generally it is, but there is a time coming when it will not be.

Now, for a good business-man and merchant who is supposed to have good judgment, backed by generous experience, what justification is there for you to engage in transactions of this kind? None. There is neither profit, interest, nor the usual banker's fee for exchange for you, but on the other hand, you take all the chances of a loss, and are your own guarantor. Transactions without profit, or show of profit, can not be predicated on sound business principles. A good rule to go by in these and all cases is this: never make a business transaction by which you can not possibly, and do not expect to be, the gainer by the sum of a fair profit or interest on your money, either directly or indirectly. Good business sense does not indorse transactions of all risk and no profit, or even safe trades without profit.

Accommodation paper and accommodation indorsers are not as abundant as they were in the last generation. Many an old man plods along to-day, poor, but wiser for his experience in this direction. But neither his experience nor wisdom have availed him in later years. That one fatal step, indorsing, caused his ruin, and his fate is the more deplorable when we consider the occasion. The present generation of business-men do not indulge in this dangerous pastime to any extent, owing, probably, to the experience and good advice of our fathers, and safer methods of doing business withal.

There are legitimate borrowers, and borrowing and lending make up a large part of our daily commerce. It is not only legitimate, but it is both necessary and profitable. The business-man with legitimate business wants is always helped. The help seeks him quite as much as he seeks it, and transactions of this class are for mutual benefit, and subserve the highest commercial purposes. But the individual who is made the subject of this chapter, the leech who fastens his suckers on his good-natured and accommodating friends, is not included in the list of legitimate borrowers. We have got him on another list, and if he should never "show up again," he will never, no, never, be missed.

DEBT VERSUS INDEPENDENCE.

Debt makes slaves of men. It robs them of their independence, of their manhood, and enslaves alike body and mind.

Within certain limits, debt, like credit—one always implying the other—is legitimate. For every dollar of credit there is a co-existent debt, and both are legitimate, proper, and conducive to the highest development of trade and commerce, as well as individual benefit. It is not, however, the legitimate function of debt and credit that we assail here; it is not their use, but their abuse, to which attention is directed.

Though debt is the result of a voluntary action to commence with, it is nevertheless grinding and full of servitude, and that of a most menial kind. Millions are kept and keep themselves in perpetual bondage, and, considering the ease with which persons can get into debt, it is not to be wondered at. Even the poor, copper-skinned laborer of Mexico knows what it is to hoe and dig all his life to make good his arrears to his priest or his employer, so that his credit will be good for the next feast day. It may be a good thing for the priest and employer to keep these poor idiots always in debt, as it keeps them in a state of bondage and subjugation, but their mission on earth would seem to be an aimless and unsatisfactory one. To get into debt is easy; to get out is far from easy. Man is born free; free from debt, at least. There is no mechanic's lien or mortgage on him at his birth. If he gets into debt later on, it must be of his own volition. The bondage is, therefore, always of his own making. The chains that bind him are of his own welding.

Slavery, as an institution, no longer exists, on this continent at least, but Abraham Lincoln's "Emancipation Proclamation" did not wipe out a species of slavery which keeps millions in servitude still. No law can reach conditions which people eagerly impose on themselves.

The ancient Jewish law contained a clause, providing, that on the day of the Jubilee, the slates should be washed clean and all debts forgiven. This provision would work well now, and in the interest of a large debtor class; not so much because its debts would be forgiven, but because creditors would be scarce and debts could not be so easily contracted.

Debts are always a burden on present efforts, since the fruits of toil go for benefits and comforts already enjoyed, instead of to be enjoyed. Mentally, men are kept on the ragged edge, scheming, conniving, aye, conspiring how to pay or not to pay their honest debts. How to pay them involves worry and discouragement, and this condition hampers the best efforts and intentions. How not to pay them incites the baser tendencies of the mind and heart. The man who is burdened with debt, who is under moral and legal obligations to his fellow-man and unable to discharge them, has ceased to be independent. His self-respect, his pride, and his sense of honor (all men have these, with rare exceptions) are made to feel a conscious degradation. What crimes, what humiliation, and what hypocrisy in all the world's history, from its beginning to the present time, may not be traced to man's indebtedness to man! Debt and bondage, in this connection, signify about the same. Watch the man who is always in debt beyond his ability to pay (it requires no philosopher's lantern to find him) and note the difference between him and his neighbor, who is master of himself. Have you ever had a debtor who would walk blocks out of his way to avoid you, or would "scoot out" by the back door when he saw you coming in by the front? Possibly you have been there yourself; though, perhaps, your case may not have been so well developed, only the symptoms, backed by a strong inclination, being present. What a power we here behold, making men slink into by-ways and alleys; making them cringe and beg as for their very existence! Think of the subtle force there capable of making us such cowards! The man who would not flinch on the battle-field, whose courage would be equal to any danger, and who would brave superior physical forces, is yet, in his creditor's presence, cowed and subdued. But it is not the creditor's presence that cows him, nor is it any force that he himself exerts. It is the debtor's consciousness of his own weakness, loss of confidence in his own rectitude; in short, it is the moral part of his nature that accuses him. Self-accusation is a formidable adversary, than whom all others are insignificant.

We have here portrayed the man in debt; let us now look at the man who is out of debt, and who purposely keeps out. Whether he possesses much or little of this world's goods, you will find in him a conscious independence, a manly self-respect before all men, and a strong personality which he has no occasion to hide or stunt; and well for every man who has learned to appreciate this state, either from experience, observation, or principle.

Within certain limits, debts are legitimate for everybody, in or out of trade. As long as they are confined to a point, and within the limits of our ability to pay at the time specified, they may be safely and advantageously incurred. But measure carefully your depth and do not go beyond it if you cherish and would maintain freedom and independence of character.

It is a favorite remark with a certain class that, "The rich are growing richer and the poor poorer." I do not think the poor are growing any poorer; they simply stay poor. There seems to be an idea prevalent among a certain class, that as one man makes himself rich, others are impoverished. There is neither logic nor reason in this. Instead of charging this disparity to any peculiar or unfair conditions of society, it is due only to natural causes. Riches and accumulations of any kind have a beginning, and the so-called poor man never makes a beginning. The methods and ways of the man who has accumulated a fortune, are not those employed by the masses. There is method in accumulating, and the great majority of the self-styled poor have none. Causes have their effects, and these are either good or bad, the alternative resting largely on our own will.

Who is it that makes the rich richer? It is the multitude of eager souls who are always getting trusted, and getting in debt, and paying three prices for the privilege. A rich man would feel that he was being robbed and ruined to pay the prices that the poor are paying. Take the "installment" plans and the innumerable "easy-payment" concerns, and who supports them? A personal friend of the writer, engaged in the business, has computed that not less than $4,000,000 annually are paid by the so-called poor people of this city and county, in excess of cash prices, for the privilege of getting things before they are able to pay for them. No man has, or can ever acquire, a competency who follows this plan. Earn first and spend afterward, is a maxim of the first importance, and one which every man must adopt if he hopes to improve his financial condition.

It is the abuse, and not the use of debt and credit that makes them a curse—to the poor, especially. *

---

* The pauper poor are not referred to here, but those people who work but never get ahead, and who style themselves " the poor " in contradistinction to those who are better off.

COMPROMISES AND EXTENSIONS.

It was the custom in the last generation for merchants to ask general extensions when they became unable to meet their obligations; but this method of getting out of financial difficulties has fallen into disuse. In our day, we ascertain what a man can afford to pay, and settle with him on a cash percentage of our claims, if we can.

Conditions are constantly changing, and what was advisable and practicable fifty years ago, does not meet the case to-day. In the first place, long time was given, and to tie up capital and accounts, by carrying customers voluntarily a year or two, was but the regular order of things. To give, then, one, two, or three years' additional time, in an emergency, with prospects of ultimate payment, seemed nothing out of the way. It was in keeping with the general tenor of things. Profits in those days were much larger than now, and this fact explains the longer terms that merchants gave and were able to give, and also furnishes reasons why extensions were practicable and judicious then, and not advisable now. In late years, an extension has invariably meant a prolongation and aggravation of the difficulties, both to debtor and creditor. Time has ceased to be the essence of the thing needed in financial embarrassments or insolvency. With larger profits and capable management, extensions might still be advisable; but the larger profits are wanting, and the fact is, that most concerns have all they can do, under fairly good conditions, to keep along, to say nothing of making up losses of the past. To ask an extension now, causes a concern's credit to be impaired and practically lost, and it is thenceforth not in position to command the lowest prices or the best service in any way, and a successful outcome can not be predicted. It is, furthermore, loaded down with interest and a large debt, which is always growing larger; it is harassed and worried, and, in short, working at tremendous disadvantage in every way. A large amount of valuable time is lost to the concern in attending to affairs of the past, instead of utilizing it to gain immediate and future results. Yesterday's profits on transactions have been determined, and no amount of time that can be bestowed on past affairs will ever make the profits of by-gone days any larger. Your time may be devoted advantageously to securing what you have made, but you can not add one iota to the amount, consequently, the more time you give to present and future operations, and the less you are obliged to give to things past, the better will be the chances of success.

The last few general extensions that come to mind, proved lamentable failures. Time only made things worse, and when the extended payments matured, affairs were more complicated and inextricable. Although, at the outset, the assets seemed to warrant paying dollar for dollar if time could be gained to convert them, many of the shrewder creditors signed the extension reluctantly. They were more willing to accept a cash offer of fifty cents on the dollar, and the subsequent outcome proved that this would have been the best thing for all interested. But the concerns would not listen to making such an offer. The property was sufficient to pay in full, and their pride and sense of honor would not permit them to compromise their indebtedness. At the final wind-up, under an assignee, the creditors did not realize even fifty cents, after losing from one to two years' time in the bargain.

The code of commercial honor which found adoption by merchants of former generations, did not countenance paying less than dollar for dollar, and compromises were looked upon as odious and dishonest. But to ask an extension of creditors, and agree to pay as fast as possible, was considered the honorable procedure for embarrassed and insolvent debtors. As a rule, the parties worked out their indebtedness in time, and this "working out" may be taken in a literal sense. But of late years, when debtors find it no longer possible to meet their obligations, they make the necessary move to compromise for cash, and this kind of settlement is generally acceptable to and preferred by creditors, provided the offer is reasonably fair, and in keeping with the insolvent's condition.

When we find merchants, as a rule, adopting certain uniform methods, we may be reasonably sure that those methods have the largest advantage on their side. We do that which pays us best, whether it be to compromise with our debtors, or anything else. That is the true principle of trade, and on this principle, compromises for cash have been found preferable to obdurateness on the part of creditors. It pays better to take fifty cents cash to-day than to take the chances of getting one dollar five or ten years hence, and perhaps not then. The fifty cents will make us fifty in five years if employed in business; on the other hand, if you should succeed in getting face value for your claim in five years, you would not be so well off then, after deducting the lawyer's fees, loss of time in looking after it, etc.; and the proportion of claims against bankrupts that are ever realized in full, is quite small. The man who has a mass of debts hanging over him, can still continue in business, and conduct it so as to evade his old creditors.

This being the experience, we say to the insolvent debtor to-day: "How much cash can you offer us on the dollar for our claim?" Of course the creditor informs himself fully as to the condition of the bankrupt's estate, and also as to the causes leading to the failure, and he is usually not slow in determining what he will take; nor does he insist on the last cent that the estate can be made to pay in the bankrupt's own hands. Creditors want a fair settlement, but are willing to leave the bankrupt in condition to continue his business, provided his course has been characterized by honesty and fair dealing.

This plan, while being fully as, if not more, advantageous than any other to the creditor, combines a humane and Christian sentiment withal.

There are a few houses that never compromise. They take either all or nothing. Some of the old Quaker houses used to refuse to sell goods to dealers who had been known at any time to settle for less than dollar for dollar. Both these cases are now rare exceptions.

Granting the wisdom, and good, practical sense of our present methods in dealing with the unfortunate debtor, we have next to consider the proper course to be pursued with regard to the dishonest and fraudulent debtor. To save ourselves annoyance, litigation, and expense, we are too much inclined to settle with him also; but in his case we should most emphatically draw the line. We should do this as a measure of self-defense and protection, and also as a warning to those whom we trust, that questionable transactions will not be lightly passed over by compromising. If creditors would adopt a uniform practice of refusing to settle with dishonest debtors, to the end that they will be kept out of trade at least, a salutary effect would be produced on the community. And more than that, whenever fraud is attempted on the creditors, there should be unanimity of sentiment and action to bring the guilty party to justice. Rather than accept the small pittance usually offered by this class, we should be willing to sacrifice it, and, instead, prosecute and punish them to the full extent of the law.

HISTORY OF CREDIT.

The oldest record we have of credit is furnished by China. Banks of deposit and discount existed there 2800 B. C., and as the existence of banks denotes a high state of development of commerce and of confidence, we may reason that credit, in that deliberate and slowly progressive country, was ages in maturing before it culminated in the establishment of banks. Eight hundred B. C. we find interest laws enacted for the protection of borrowers, and 500 B. C. the Chinese Government issued paper money. We find in the earliest history of Egypt and India credit transactions recorded. We read of the Hebrew women 1500 B. C. going out into the wilderness glittering with jewelry and trinkets borrowed from their Egyptian neighbors; nor is this mentioned as a novel occurrence.

History gives us no clue as to when and where the first actual credit transaction took place. That this occurred at an early period when man was still in a semi-civilized state, and incapable of reducing traditions and events to writing, we may readily take for granted. The most ancient writers to whose works we have access, lead us to conclude, by inference at least, that credit was not only contemporaneous with them, but even more ancient than they.

Clauses pertaining to contracts, debt, mortgage, etc., were contained in the Jewish law, as well as that of India and China, and a national bankruptcy court seems to have been as much a necessity then as now, only they called it by different names. One of the grand provisions of the Jubilee demanded that "the slate" be washed clean, and all debts be forgiven at stated intervals.

In Athens and other commercial centers of Greece, the credit system was not unknown. The rights of capitalists were strictly guarded, though they were heavily taxed. Money was obtainable, and money-lenders were numerous, but interest was high. Indorsing for one another seems to have been customary then as in modern times, for we find laws pertaining to the liability of the indorser. They had marine insurance and probably fire insurance companies. Cargoes were insured, and vessels were burned or shipwrecked for the sake of the insurance money then, as ever since.

In Rome, also, the credit system flourished. There were many rich people, composed mainly of the nobles, who never turned a deaf ear to the poor applicant—if he had good security. But even without this, the noble lord was tolerably safe, since he had not only a hand in making the laws, but the right of enforcing them to suit his lordship's own ideas of justice. We are told that "torture, slavery, and imprisonment with hard labor, in a private jail some two stories beneath the banquet hall of the illustrious usurer, were the lot of all delinquents, and well for them if they ever got out of his clutches again." With prospects like these staring one in the face, it must have required considerable nerve to become a borrower.

In feudal Europe, neither credit nor commerce attained to any growth. For many centuries there was complete stagnation in the sciences, arts, and commerce. That period in the history of the Caucasian race was unsettled and full of turbulence. The only law that prevailed was that of "might." We read of credit being given, but it lacked the essence of a free-will transaction. Often the lender was not a willing party to the transaction, but the alternative was not to be thought of. It was simply a choice as between two evils. Practically, borrowing was disguised robbery. Rich Jews, wealthy provinces and cities, were alike called upon for loans by the feudal lords, and it was either to grant the request voluntarily or be compelled to do so at the point of the sword, or something worse. Sometimes the loans were repaid in a left-handed manner by granting the creditor special privileges, but they were rarely paid back in money. A demand for the return of a loan would have been more likely to meet with dry blows from the princely borrower and his minions, than with payment in hard cash.

In the Europe of the Middle Ages, we find the first banks established by the rich trading centers of Genoa, Venice, Hamburg, and Bremen. From the time of the establishment of these, we may date the growth of commerce and credit. As banks can not flourish in communities where confidence does not exist, we must assume that the conditions in Europe had undergone a change for the better. But we must not infer that the functions of banks were the same then as now. They accommodated the public mainly in one way, namely, as repositories of gold and silver, plate, jewels, valuable documents belonging to the wealthy few, and to the State or smaller municipalities. That these deposits represented enormous value must be allowed from the fact that, at various times, the cupidity of revolutionary armies in adjacent States was aroused and frequent assaults were made on Bern, Genoa, Venice, and Amsterdam for the purpose of laying hands on the vast treasures held by the banks of those cities.

Holland in the seventeenth century had better credit than France or England, and, up to the reign of Queen Anne, she continued to be the first commercial nation. After that, England was in the ascendency, and has maintained it ever since, and its credit, at home and abroad, from that time to this, has always been the wonder and amazement of other nations. We are told that "the Persian embassadors of hardly more than a century ago, could never comprehend the national debt of Great Britain; they talked much of it, they questioned their English friends, and sent home voluminous dispatches on the subject of the fabulous liability of the Britons. But when they were shown the park of artillery at Woolwich, and heard the roar of ordnance on a field day, they refused to hear further explanation of the debt, declaring that the 'British Government had cannon and gunpowder enough to blow debt and creditors into infinite space,' and that, under these favorable circumstances, no demand for payment was possible."

They solved the problem in precisely the same manner that the despots of old would have done. Not even the legal form of repudiation of interest or principal would have been deemed necessary by them.

We are shown that a high state of credit marks a corresponding degree of civilization. Savages and the ruder tribes of uncivilized countries hardly know what credit means, and have no word even expressive of its meaning. Only where probity and ownership of property exists, and where rightful possession is defined by a higher law than that of the individual standard, can credit flourish. In the matter of property and ownership, the savage is like a child; everything within his reach he appropriates, and neither scruples nor asks questions. Of what we term honor, the savage has none, and truth he is a stranger to—with strangers particularly.

In all civilized communities we find credit, but its use is found to vary according to the intelligence and education of the people. Credit is given liberally by the Chinese, we are told. They are thrifty in their way, and understand the accumulating properties of little grains of sand better than any other people. They are also the greatest swindlers, in a small way, in the world; though in their commercial transactions with one another, they are said to be very honest. No bankrupt laws exist, but debtors are liable to corporal punishment. Not paying one's debts is a disgrace in China, and the debtor is practically "drummed out" of business. The whole nation "settles up" at New Year's Day, which comes usually in February. It is said that China never had a panic, and that in times of famine or failure of crops, the Government furnishes liberal aid to the sufferers, although recent events do not corroborate this statement.

In all European countries we find credit, but its use is more or less restricted in different localities. In Italy nearly everything is done for cash; the same in Spain; on the other hand, in Russia and Turkey twelve months is usually given, even on articles of prime necessity. The difference in the customs of these nations is probably owing to climatic conditions and occupations. In Western Europe, we find from three to six months' credit rulable.

Credit-giving is manifestly one of man's inventions, for we can not find that Nature ever established the custom. Nature gives us no credit. We must work first and eat afterward, and she is inexorable in her strict adherence to these terms. Man, however, is more pliant and accommodating in his methods, and is subject to a corresponding degree of disappointment and failure in his affairs. In dealing with Nature, we must first till the soil and sow the seed before we can eat of the abundance of the golden grain. Without this, the fields can not be persuaded to yield the harvest. The hunter must trudge to secure the game; even the wild fruit and the shell fish make toil necessary for their obtainment. Thus we see that Nature is firm and holds us steadily to fixed conditions, and it is no doubt well that she does so.

"Credit has an aptitude for good and evil; it can be benign or malignant in turn, but its existence is a sure mark of progress in the social scale. How it slowly ripened, bearing fruit in the shape of stocks, bonds, bank and government notes, loans, and mercantile credits would be difficult to trace. We exchange our earnings for the flimsy bits of paper with a trust that is most wonderful, and the wonder is that credulity does not oftener outstrip performance. But this modern credit is the creation of our own confidence, withal, and in the course of its development has struck deep roots in the very heart of the State."

"Credit is two-faced and may be employed to our benefit or injury according as its potent aid is invoked. With a good foundation for our business to stand on, backed by brains and energy, it may be used advantageously within proper limits. The danger lies in too great reliance on its good offices. It is often looked upon as an inexhaustible quarry, ever ready to yield to our wants, but apt to fail us when most needed."

Credit, like fire, when carefully handled is of incalculable service.

OUR CREDIT SYSTEM.

Some one has aptly said: "Commerce is the offspring and at the same time the support of civilization." Wherever we find the one, we always find the other. Commerce came with the growth of civilization, the latter being the cause, and the former the natural result. This we must accept as a fact, although to day we might almost be inclined to believe that commerce was the cause, and civilization the effect.

But commerce does not stand as the agent or representative of civilization in doing this grand work of civilizing and educating. While she performs this work, and does it well, it is foreign to her real purpose and apart from her mission. The purpose of commerce is not of a philanthropic nature; it has no such motive. Self-interest and the hope of personal aggrandizement are its incentives, and these furnish the motive-power for its penetrating and aggressive tendencies.

Thus we see that civilization and commerce are so closely allied that it is difficult to determine which one of the two leads or follows. When we consider the relationship of commerce and credit, we find the line of demarkation even more indistinct. They are of simultaneous growth, and the existence of one always implies, and is indispensable to the other.

It might be argued that commerce could exist without credit. Possibly, on a very limited scale. Every commercial or mercantile transaction is based on credit at some point. Your confidence causes you to rely on statements made, and you credit these statements. You may buy a barrel of St. Louis flour, and pay the cash for it, but there is a credit implied, nevertheless. What makes you pay the cash for the flour before you have actually examined the contents of the barrel, weighed it on your own scales, and satisfied yourself from other sources that the flour was made in St. Louis, and not in Minneapolis, as claimed? You see, even in our cash transactions, credit is given. In the above case the buyer gives all the credit and takes all the chances, whereas, in the ordinary credit transactions, the flour being sold on time, both buyer and seller give credit. They have mutual confidence in one another that each will do as he agrees. In the earliest stages of civilization, commerce had no existence, and credit or its synonym, mutual confidence, was unknown. Exchanges were made of one commodity for another, but traffic of this kind is called barter, and does not reach the dignity of being called commerce or trade. The North American trapper takes. beads, showy trinkets, and gewgaws with him when he visits the wild tribes of the West and North, and these he exchanges with the Indians for their furs. Both get what they bargained for on the spot, and neither credit nor confidence enters into the transaction.

But to follow the course and growth of commerce and credit from its incipiency and from a stage of barter, when honor and mutual confidence were still undeveloped qualities in man, to that of our present state of commerce and credit and universal confidence, would lead us outside the domain of a practical business treatise, and open up a field more in keeping with the labors of the historian. Man's means of support must necessarily at all times have been an all-important element in his condition. His education, progress, and development are so dependent on and so closely interwoven with the means afforded him for support, that commerce, which for ages has furnished that means to a greater or lesser degree in the different epochs of the world's history, must have exerted an all-pervading influence and powerful stimulus on the welfare and possibilities of nations and of men.

In no country is credit so cheap or so high as in the United States. It is said to be cheap because it is so easily obtained, or high, because capital goes out freely and is willing to take its chances on all manner of enterprises, so long as they offer prospective returns for the investment. It is the exception here when a man is denied credit for any ordinary or even extraordinary business wants.

The marvelous progress and development of this country is the wonder of the world, and our own amazement finds no limit; but as a single factor in helping to bring about this condition, our credit system, extending as it does into every nook and corner of this great continent and beyond it, is no less worthy of remark, and commands the admiration of those capable of a just conception of its importance. Why this willingness and eagerness of everybody to trust everybody should exhibit itself more in this country than in others, is not to be reasoned out on the assertion made sometimes that credit is highest where population is densest, and vice versa. On that theory all European countries would enjoy much higher credit than we, which is not, however, substantiated by the facts. If density of population caused credit to be more easily obtained, it would follow that credit ought to be dispensed with a more liberal hand to-day than it was fifty years ago, which, also, is not the case. In fact, the long-time credits of that period, when six and twelve months were regularly given to traders in the far West and South, with hardly any communication except when buyers visited the markets, required rather greater confidence than is exhibited, or would be considered warrantable, to-day. The curtailment of the time in late years, we will admit not to be due to a lesser degree of confidence, but to smaller margins, which has necessitated turning capital over oftener than once or twice a year, and also to the fact that the trading community has more capital at command. But could confidence possibly reach a higher limit than when the New York merchants, previous to the era of railroads and the telegraph, trusted their goods out to the far distant Territories, with only stage-coach facilities for reaching them and where the debtor was known to have all the advantages on his side? It is evident that we must look for the cause of our wonderful credit system in other directions, and not attribute it to density of population.

Credit flourishes in proportion as people have confidence in each other; but confidence does not come of itself. What creates it with us, is, that greater opportunity is afforded for making money, and this, joined to our natural ability as traders and aptitude in improving opportunites, is what gives us faith in each other. Every man with moderate ability can make money here; he can hold his own, at least, and support his family out of his business, and there is reasonable expectation of success in every legitimate undertaking. Our inherent individual honesty we will rate no higher than that of other nations, and placing all nations on a par on this score, we have this additional advantage over all, that money is, and can be, more easily made here, and this is an all important consideration in the minds of those who have money or goods to let out. If a man were known to be ever so honest, credit would not be extended to him if his chances of success seemed doubtful. We are only willing to risk our capital when we find a reasonable assurance that the borrower or debtor will be able to repay it at the appointed time, with interest or profit. This assurance is felt here to a much greater degree than in other countries, and has been built up by the prestige of past experience.

We are recognized the world over as a nation of traders. To deserve this encomium and to build up this reputation for ourselves, has settled us in the conviction that we possess superior advantages, as well as talents, in our methods of money making. These are the elements that contribute to the development of our credit system, and capital, consisting either of money or goods, feels not only safe in the return of the principal, but has every assurance also of interest or profit. This furnishes the fundamental principles on which credit is established, nor will it flourish under adverse conditions.

In countries where we find a high rate of interest rulable, and where 5 per cent. per month is demanded for the use of capital on the most available securities, we shall always find insecurity of property and a doubtful feeling as to the ability of the borrower to return the loan at the appointed time. Capital, on the other hand, with us is more productive at from 5 to 7 per cent. per annum, it being constantly kept earning, and at this rate is always loanable with the utmost security and without great risk or anxiety to the lender. The larger the risk that men take, the larger will be the charges exacted. The hope of large gain is always attended with proportionately great risk. "High interest means bad security," is an old maxim.

The credit system may be said to have been a growth of necessity, like other systems and conditions. The growth of civilization and industry made it indispensable, and it kept on growing with the progress of commercial punctuality and integrity, and wherever it finds the aliment of its growth, it flourishes and can not be destroyed. Long before it attained its present magnitude and extension, it had sent out many vigorous shoots in various countries. In a work by Stephen Colwell we find mention made of the fairs, so prevalent in Europe in the Middle Ages, some of which continue even down to our time, and that payments at these fairs were made, to a large extent, by setting off debts against debts. "Men learned to pay their debts with their credits, and this mode of payment only disappeared as the progress of the credit system and the growth of cities absorbed both the business and the payment of the fairs." Every debt implying a credit, the fact was revealed that no one could better employ his credit than in paying his debts. This required no money, and was, therefore, not only economical, but free from innumerable risks and trouble inseparably connected with payments in money.

Our clearing houses and exchanges, our banking business, and our commercial and financial transactions, are all conducted on precisely the same principle. Jones borrows money at the bank and the amount is placed to his credit. He owes Smith, and gives him a check on his bank. Smith deposits it (in the same bank perhaps), and the check is credited to Smith and charged to Jones. No money, or actual cash, is handled in the transaction. Credits are thus used to pay debts; but before this function of credit can be utilized to the uttermost, as we see it to-day,. a fully-developed credit system and mutual confidence are absolutely necessary.

All our large enterprises, our large corporations, and undertakings of both a private and public character, are due to, and have been possible only through, the medium of our credit system. The capital to further and operate these enterprises is contributed, in a large measure, by the many, although a few large capitalists generally take the lead. But both small and large investors have confidence and are willing and eager to intrust their accumulations to the management of others, in the expectation of fair returns. To this confidence, to this facility for obtaining credit, it is due that companies can be founded for purposes the most useful and beneficial. It is not the individual ownership of money, but credit, that "bridges the morass, spans the land with iron rails and the sea with copper wires, and is building, spinning, making, and gathering all that can be built, spun, made, or gathered."

The banking business of a country furnishes the best index to its credit, both national and individual, and to the confidence existing among its people in one another. To foreigners our methods of banking seem loose and insecure, and to an English or Continental banker, accustomed to the precautions used in his country, we appear, at first glance, most reckless. American bankers trust out their funds with the same freedom as does the merchant his goods, and not unfrequently loans for business uses are made solely on the borrower's individual responsibility and reputation, without other security or guarantee of second or third parties as indorsers.

Every bank customer, of any standing whatever, being thus readily and cheerfully accommodated with loans to an amount within keeping with his capital and business, the customer, if he be a merchant or manufacturer, can increase his business to the extent of his ability to become a borrower, and in this wise trade is greatly facilitated and the country benefited. What he trusts out on the one hand, beyond the limit of his own capital, he borrows on the other hand from the banks, and though he pays 6 per cent. per annum for the money, he is the gainer by the difference between the interest paid and the profits secured. And the large accumulation of our loanable funds always finds a ready demand from this source. Bankers are as eager to find borrowers as borrowers are to find bankers. In times of panic and depression the banker is forced, much against his will and inclination, to call in and reduce his loans as a matter of safety. When money commands the highest rate of interest, which is evidence of loss or want of confidence, bankers find it necessary to be most conservative, and dare not avail themselves of the opportunity of making the larger gains. Although the rate of interest is higher, they earn less money, as only a small proportion of the capital and deposits can be loaned out with safety. In ordinary times, on the contrary, the minimum reserve only need be kept on hand, thus allowing a much larger proportion of the bank's funds and deposits to be used. Whether banks feel called upon to keep the maximum or minimum reserve, whereby a stringent or an easy money market is largely caused, is simply an evidence of favorable or unfavorable conditions. In times of panic, banks get the credit of making "confusion worse confounded" by calling in their loans and refusing new ones; but banks are really responsible for this in but a small measure. It is the depositors, composed of people who are not actively engaged in business, and who easily take fright, who cause the stringency by loss of confidence in the safety of the banks and who consequently withdraw their money for safe-keeping in an old stocking. The withdrawal from circulation, and from the loanable funds, of the aggregate of all these small deposits, is a matter beyond the control of the banks, and loans and deposits, in the hands of others, not bankers, are likewise subject to be called in from the same general cause.

High credit is indicative of universal confidence, and increases the productiveness of a country. This confidence is what keeps the savings and earnings of the people in circulation, and whoever accumulates a savings fund, be it ever so small, deposits or invests it where it will be used in producing and earning, either directly or indirectly. Outside of the pocket money of the people, money is not kept locked up or hidden away as it used to be, except during times of financial distress. In this generation, and in all commercial countries, money is esteemed more for its earning capacity than for the thing itself; in other words, a larger proportion of the people's money assumes the character of capital, and the difference between the two terms is, that capital is money (or wealth) employed in producing and earning, while money, not productively employed, is not capital.

The miser is a relic of a period when hoarding and hiding money and valuables was necessary for their safe-keeping, and when a condition of universal confidence of man in man had no existence. The miser has no confidence in anybody or anything, except the glittering gold and silver coins themselves, though latterly we have read of finding greenbacks actually stowed away among the effects of defunct misers; but such a stretch of confidence as this, in even "Uncle Sam's scrip," is evidence, surely, of miserly degeneracy, and of a weakened mind.

The money hoarded and hidden by the miser is taken out of circulation and ceases to be productive. In this light, a community of misers and a community of barbarians or Hottentots, by neither of whom mutual confidence is understood, would produce about the same relative results and conditions, inasmuch as neither community would contribute to productiveness or development of natural resources.

The difference between this condition, without credit, and our actual condition, with the function of credit fully developed, is simply the difference between a condition of ignorance and barbarism and that of the highest type of civilization and development of the human race.

CREDIT: ITS RELATION TO CAPITAL AND LABOR.

The natural and logical order in which these great factors in our industrial system range themselves, is labor, capital, and credit.

Labor is the source whence *all* wealth is derived. It is the prime factor, and of necessity precedes capital and credit; for without its performance, neither the one nor the other could have existence. Wealth represents the surplus of labor performed in excess of the requirements to maintain life; but our aggregate wealth is not an exact or even approximate measure of the product of labor. Natural agents and causes frequently aid in augmenting capital where it already exists; but such augmentation is due, nevertheless, to the impulse given by labor, both past and present. Whatever property of value we may possess, is certain to have required a certain amount of labor to be expended in its production. This labor may, or may not, have been performed by us, but that an equivalent has been rendered for our possessions, at some time and by someone, is an indisputable fact, and whether we are the fortunate heirs to an estate, or have found the money, does not alter the case.

To produce food for our maintenance requires labor, though only a small portion of our time need be sacrificed in toiling, where mere existence is the sole object of life, as with the ruder tribes of men of to-day, or with our own race in its pre-civilized state. The performance of labor, like its employment, both having for their object present and future benefits, is the outgrowth of civilization and education. Savages do not labor in the sense that we do; i. e., work to-day for benefits to be derived hereafter. The law of self-sacrifice—self-sacrificing the present for the future—is, like the moral law, an evidence of a higher development, whose threshold the savage has not yet crossed. And in this respect a wide divergence is noticeable among members of the same society or class, and to which is attributable the difference in their respective social conditions. "Take no heed of the morrow," is accepted in its literal sense, and the injunction is as religiously obeyed by a large portion of the civilized community as by barbarians, who never heard of it.

Though rich in everything which bountiful Nature could supply, this continent was left undisturbed and undeveloped in its primitive grandeur, waiting for the hand of labor to make the transformation from a great wilderness to a garden of plenty for eager and hungry millions. Less than three centuries ago, what now constitutes the United States had not the commercial value that many a New England or

Western village boasts of to-day; but the wonderful change was not wrought by a miracle; it came through labor, and labor only.

The Indian, though lord of all he surveyed, and his domain was large, had no care except for immediate wants. Game and water were within easy reach, and to satisfy hunger and thirst for the time being was his sole concern. Generation after generation found him in precisely the same condition. There was no thought for the morrow, and thrift was as unknown to him as were civilization and education. Not willing to make a present sacrifice of his comfort for a future gain, he never produced or acquired anything, and the resources of fertile plain and the earth's hidden treasures were left unmolested, waiting for him who would sow in the spring and wait till harvest-time for his wages.

To say that the Indian did not labor would be untrue; but his labor consisted in simply providing for his actual wants, and no more. The Indian would rather work for fifty cents a day and receive his wages at night, than to work for thirty dollars a month with deferred payment for his toil.

Labor performed in excess of physical wants from day to day, represents capital, but it may not assume the function of capital in our own hands. If, for instance, the excess earnings are applied to surround ourselves with extra comforts, to the betterment of our moral, mental, and physical conditions, we have lost possession of the tangible capital to be used again by us; but, the aggregate wealth of the world has been enhanced. Thus, we see, that the man who labors one or two more hours beyond actual necessity, is a creator of capital or wealth, which is subsequently used, by him or others, in further production and accumulation.

The modern conditions of our social and industrial structure have brought about the necessity of a division into bodily and mental labor. Brain-work, which furnishes the directive power must be classed as labor, as much as the work performed by the hands and muscles of the body. Both are necessary for the successful operations of business, and when made coöperative, the largest results are obtained, in fact, no great results can be achieved without yoking the two forces together. The superior workman is known by the force and quality of mind that direct his hands, and, under all circumstances, a combination of the two enhances the value of each. The value and potentiality of mental labor exclusively depend on circumstances. Where a man's subsistence must be toiled for by himself, brain-work, or directive power alone, would accomplish nothing. A certain amount of manual labor must be performed to result in the production of food or anything else; but in the modern methods of doing business the division is not only practicable, but economical, and subserves the best interests of all concerned. The capitalist, by reason of his natural and acquired ability, gives sufficient directive force in a few hours daily to keep 100 or 1,000 hands employed. He plans the work while others execute it, and each one is equal to his task without undue hardship.

"Capital is the representative of the product of labor already performed." This definition is given by John Stuart Mill in his "Principles of Political Economy," and applies equally to our individual and to the aggregate wealth of nations.

There is a distinction made between wealth, capital, and money. The last two are always part of the first, but wealth is not always capital, nor can all our wealth be converted into money at one time, since we have only about one dollar in money to every thirty possessed by us in property; yet this proportion is found amply sufficient to facilitate our exchanges, and that is the only purpose which money serves.

Wealth is defined as consisting of anything useful or agreeable, which nature does not afford gratuitously, and for which some other form of property would be given in exchange.

Capital is that portion of wealth devoted to

productive uses, and employed in any form of industry for the purpose of making profit or interest, or otherwise adding to the principal.

Money constitutes a considerable part of our capital, but only a small portion of our wealth, and of all property it is the most available, since it affords instantaneous command over objects of our desire. It represents the net result of a series of transactions which are considered completed only when we have succeeded in converting them into money. But money is not necessarily capital, although in this age a larger proportion than formerly has assumed that function; in fact, all our money or circulating medium may be considered to be productively employed and be termed capital, that portion used for pocket or spending money excepted, of course. To illustrate when money is not capital, suppose a case where a man deposits $1,000 in a vault for safe-keeping. Being withdrawn from circulation and earning or producing nothing, it ceases to be capital; but it still remains wealth. It has been robbed, temporarily, of its legitimate function of production, but continues to possess the quality of being exchangeable with the utmost facility for things desired, and is therefore in the best form to be used with the least inconvenience. This same $1,000, the moment it is released from its hiding-place and used in manufacturing or any business whatsoever, whereby production is effected or assisted, immediately assumes the function of capital again; nor need it be directly employed by the owner himself. Lending it to another on interest results in its productive employment, since no one could afford or be willing to borrow and pay for the use of money, unless he expected to use it and make money by the operation himself. Having thus briefly explained, intelligibly, I hope, the difference between wealth, capital, and money, we will take up the subject of capital, with which we are more especially concerned.

Capital is the result of accumulation, and an accumulation once made becomes a permanent fund for productive operations, present and future. We may take as an illustration, the case of a small farmer under different and distinct phases. One is given a piece of land which he works, and raises all that he needs for bare subsistence, but no more. He has nothing to sell or to exchange, and one year finds him no better off than its predecessor. The labor performed is in exact proportion to the bodily requirements of the man. No accumulation is here effected, and capital is not produced. This is practically the case of the savage. On the other hand, the farmer who labors more hours, and who has a surplus of product beyond his own wants to exchange for stock, machinery, or for clearing or obtaining additional land, is a producer of capital.

Having, by his labor and industry, reaped a harvest which not only yields the means of subsistence for himself for a year, but enables him also to provide for another man's subsistence, he has made himself a capitalist to that extent. We will suppose, now, that the farmer discovers on his land a coal or iron mine. The surplus product of his previous year's labor makes it possible for him to employ another man to develop this natural resource, while he devotes himself to acquiring another year's sustenance to enable him to prosecute his work of development beyond the present year.

We here have the capitalist, and we see that he has made himself such, simply by the performance of labor in excess of his personal needs. He has accumulated a fund, consisting of food in this case, which represents to him and others an exchange value either for acquiring other objects or other men's labor. The inference would be that the producer of food is the originator and principal source of all capital and wealth, and that labor in other departments, not directly productive of food, owes the possibility of its existence to the tiller of the soil, and this is logically true.

In the animal and insect world we find "capitalists" at certain seasons of the year, and in some instances at all times. The squirrel collects what he deems a sufficient supply of acorns to carry him through the winter; the bee and the ant show prodigious energy in providing for future wants. We call this instinct; but it were well for a portion of mankind were they to exchange man's higher estate of reason for simple instinct.

Most of us can earn enough in four hours per day to sustain life and procure the absolute necessaries. Some are content with this; others are willing to labor a little more for what special indulgences it may provide; but those, only, who labor with a desire and for the purpose of having a surplus left out of their earnings, become capitalists. We often hear it said that our millionaires have not performed labor or rendered an equivalent in labor for their possessions; in fact, that no labor at all has been performed for it. If this were true, and capital or wealth was the creation of a mental process, simply and purely, the more of such creative geniuses this country could boast of, the better it would be, most assuredly. But the fact is, that not one dollar of capital exists that does not represent an equivalent in work performed by someone, whether it be in the hands of the laborer, the farmer, the merchant, or the millionaire. The men who live by their "wits" or who make speculation their business, live on the produce and the labor of their fellow-men. While it does not appear to be right that one man should be allowed to live on the fruits of another's efforts, it is yet a fact of human life, as much as that the sun shines on the just and unjust alike. Notwithstanding the wailings of a certain discontented class, the laws governing commerce and society, and man's intercourse with man, are nevertheless fixed and immutable, so far as the individual is concerned, adjusting themselves, however, to the varying conditions and improvement of the race, and in this respect only, differing from the laws of Nature.

Reverting to the subject of speculators and men living by their "wits," as we say, they are not producers, and in no sense can they be said to be a helpful addition to our industrial forces. They live on what others have already produced, and aim to appropriate as much of this product of others as their ingenuity or superior sagacity enables them to. They can live and thrive only where the earnings and savings of others are in process of accumulation. Stanley has not reported finding them in his African tour, and not until others have gone there and reared the industrial structure, will the speculator be induced to bring his special talent to that market. Capital must first have existence, before men can live on each other or be of any use to each other, and only as man advances in the social scale so that he will work and save, will he become a potent factor in his own welfare and contribute to that of the community.

To quote from the Political Economy of Mr.

Mill: "All capital originally is the result of saving, and a saving once made, becomes a permanent fund to be used in endless productive operations, each operation being self-sustained and paying a profit besides." To enjoy the comforts and luxuries of life; to be independent—in short, to be in the possession of wealth—is the goal of our ambition; but however ardently we may desire these things, the goal is not reached by simply wishing. We must *work* and *save*.

"Credit is not equivalent to the creation of capital, but it helps to make capital more productive by being transferred to hands more competent to employ it efficiently." Credit is not an independent factor, although it appears that in the minds of many, credit is the equal of capital and capable of performing all its functions independently. But not one dollar of credit can be given unless a saving and accumulation to that extent have been effected and have tangible existence in what is termed capital.

The function of credit is not production, but to *aid* production and distribution. This it does, and to this is owing the greater remuneration enjoyed by capital where the conditions in a community warrant a liberal dispensation of credit. Not all men nor even all owners of capital are qualified by education or inclination to engage in productive operations, but they seek to employ their capital, nevertheless, and by becoming partners or lenders and joining forces with men of experience and energy, they are enabled thus to reap part of the profits arising from such combinations. But it must be borne in mind that the same dollar can be used in but one operation at a time. For one man to give another part of his capital is an unconditional surrender; to lend is a conditional surrender or transfer; but in each case the original owner has diminished his power of production in the exact ratio that the borrower's has been increased. From a superficial view it might appear that although A has parted with his capital to B, he can use the securities received from B and not be hindered in engaging in business himself. But this only changes the personality of lender and borrower, for B would then be using C's capital instead of A's. Now, in our actual business transactions the personality of lender and borrower, creditor and debtor, is constantly changing; but a first principle governs each and all—at some point every credit transaction must be represented by capital and be based upon it.

We can readily see that industry is limited by capital, and this limitation holds equally true of credit, although it might seem that our credit-giving capacity was greater than our capital. For instance, when A buys $10 worth of sugar and sells it at $11 on credit, his credit-giving capacity would seem to exceed the capital invested. But right here we must not lose sight of a very important factor in the creation of capital, namely, labor. The dollar added to the original investment represents A's labor as distributor or agent.

There is and has been at all times and among all classes of men, not excepting legislators and even prominent business-men, an erroneous conception of the nature of credit, it being looked upon as a creation possessing inherent powers and attributes, and capable of performing functions which it can only acquire by a transfer of the thing it represents, viz., capital. The inflationists, previous to 1879, comprised a very respectable faction, both in numbers and general intelligence. They insisted that the nation's promise to pay was all-sufficient without reference to its ability, based on property (national wealth) to secure or ultimately redeem. In holding to this theory they manifestly ignored the fundamental law governing the simplest business transactions. A nation's claim to credit, like that of an individual's, must always be based on property; otherwise this claim will not be recognized, whatever may be decreed by legislative enactments. Our gold and silver certificates pass current because we have confidence in the assurance that the government has gold and silver coin or bullion in its treasury vaults. While the notes are in circulation we know that the property they represent is held intact for the security of the holder, and this furnishes the basis of our confidence in and ready acceptance of them.

MERCANTILE AGENCIES.

Since the mercantile agency is the direct outgrowth and is so inseparably connected with and dependent for its support on our credit system, and since, also, it has come to be recognized as an indispensable adjunct to present conditions and methods of doing business, it may not be amiss to give a brief outline of its origin, growth, and present status.

The Mercantile Agency System was first conceived and put into operation in New York City about the year 1837. The great commercial crisis of that year led certain parties conversant with mercantile affairs and the credit system, as it then existed, to attempt the introduction of a method whereby the mercantile interests might find better protection and be surrounded with greater safeguards. With this end in view, and backed by leading houses for whose special benefit the scheme was more directly devised, a bureau for collecting information was opened by a Mr. Church. This was the beginning of our present Mercantile Agency System, and up to that time nothing had been attempted in this direction.

The larger houses in those days employed commercial travelers, who managed to get around to their customers once or twice a year; but the object of these annual or semiannual visits was more to cultivate acquaintance and strengthen the relationship between buyer and seller. An estimate of customers, both as to character and responsibility, was thus formed, and their limit of credit, which we take to have been almost unlimited, was established. Though good, so far as it went, this plan was not alone expensive, but thoroughly inadequate to the needs of the times. Commerce was growing and extending in every direction, and new applicants for credit were constantly pouring in from every quarter, and of these nothing was or could be known, of course. To trust, or not to trust, however, must be decided at once. There was no agency to consult or telegraph to make use of while the customer was being entertained and shown through the stock. Under such circumstances these were both momentous and difficult questions to decide; but as every condition creates and develops its own defense and safeguard, so the merchants of those days were equal to the emergency by means of another school of training, differing entirely from our present methods.

Most of us can remember when it was the custom of merchants, from all parts of the country, to repair to the metropolis once a year, at least, for the two-fold purpose of settling up and buying new stocks. This custom brought the New York merchant in personal contact with his customers, both old and new, and developed in him a faculty for determining character and judging men and human nature, that has been largely lost to modern business science, and which constituted the essence of a thorough business-training fifty years ago.

Looking back to this and still remoter periods in our commercial history, the law of compensation is brought to our minds with full force. We enjoy great advantages to-day, and would not willingly give up the least of our conveniences; but we have surely made a sacrifice for them, to which the old-time merchant could never become reconciled. A customer in those days stood in the light of a friend—even a warm personal friend. Buyer and seller, after their relationship was once established, did not meet simply for what they could make out of each other. The Southern or Western trader combined pleasure with business when making his annual visit to the metropolis, and meeting his business friends periodically was his vacation and recreation. The merchant in turn received him with the most cordial handshake and generous hospitality, for which New York merchants were renowned. A customer then, once secured, could be relied on for continued patronage. There was real, genuine friendship, and this was the foundation on which the integrity and honor of buyer and seller mutually rested. Nor was this mutual confidence often *willfully* abused.

Laws for the collection of debts were on the statute books, and in some States were quite severe, but as regards any benefit to the creditor, they were practically a dead letter. We find in the literature of that period, as late as 1847, a suggestion, emanating from some of the larger houses in New York, that the laws for the collection of debts be abolished altogether, and that dependence be placed entirely on the honor and honesty of the buyers. To collect by process of law from a trader in the Territorial governments of the then wild West, was, of course, impracticable from a business standpoint, if not impossible. The *Dry Goods Record* of that time also favored the repeal of the collection laws, and its arguments were, that in the absence of any legal redress for the creditor, a higher moral responsibility would be developed in the buyer by trusting entirely to his moral sense, and having it so understood. Although the laws remained in force, the argument was not altogether illogical for those days, though now it would be impracticable. Yet we do find, even to-day, in the liquor business, for instance, credit given on a large scale to dealers residing in States where the collection of liquor bills can not be enforced by law. Such is the confidence of man in man, that credit will flourish even without any protection from the law.

Taking up again the origin of the agencies, we find the purpose of its promoters to have been to collect and obtain information of the financial standing and responsibility of traders doing business with New York merchants, and it was mainly in the interest of a few of the larger houses that the agency undertook the work. The idea having much in it to recommend it, the list of patrons soon increased, and with it, the scope and value of the institution were increased also.

The first reference-book was issued about the year 1840. While the list of names furnished was not large, the information was reliable. It was not so much an effort for quantity of material as of quality, and in this respect the value of the agency was not enhanced by time and experience. Competition presently entered the field, and this may be held responsible for the subsequent degeneracy and drifting away from the original plan and high resolve of its promoters. The success of the first agency soon attracted others to the field, some short-lived and others to stay, and ere long there was keen competition for patronage, and efforts, not to out-do, but to out-show each other were the result. Instead of giving the public honest and conscientious work, it resulted in lists without regard to reliability of statements. As long as only one was in the field, the most reliable service was sought to be given, and competition can not be said to have worked beneficially in this instance.

The promoters originally sought to supply only authoritative information, when information was given at all, and this policy should have been rigidly adhered to, for it is not quantity that business-men want, if it is at the expense of reliability. No report at all is better than an incorrect one, and if the agencies would follow this suggestion more uniformly, they would give vastly better service to the business community. Like a general storekeeper, who tries to keep everything because the nature of his business implies supplying every want of his customers, so the agencies undertake to answer all inquiries to satisfy subscribers, thus appearing to give them service for their money.

Yet, considering how much they undertake and how much is asked of them, it is surprising, that they render as acceptable service as they do, especially when we consider the difficulties under which they labor. First, it is incompetency and want of business knowledge and tact of the correspondents. Second, carelessness and indifference of correspondents to their work, in which they have no especial interest, and which they perform, in a large measure, gratuitously. Thirdly, personal favoritism or prejudice is apt to sway the correspondent's mind, consciously, sometimes, and unconsciously at others, and so a long list of difficulties might be enumerated which operate against the agency. Local reporters for agencies rarely get paid for their services, except in an indirect way. Even when under direct pay, it is not remunerative enough to command great talent or much time.

But notwithstanding all the shortcomings of the system, and with all its glaring defects, it is, nevertheless, a permanent institution with the American business-public, and has come to stay. Notably among the agencies of to-day, R. G. Dun & Co. and Bradstreet may be cited, and as money-making institutions they have been very successful, and this necessarily proves their popularity and usefulness. But we cheerfully give them credit, also, for constantly improving their service and of appropriating a fair share of their immense earnings toward the perfecting of their systems. Infallibility is not one of the things chargeable to them to any alarming extent, but that the reports of to-day are a great improvement over those of twenty years ago, or even ten, is cause for much encouragement. Within the last few years the agency has been accorded a place in the business community of this country at least, and by reason of this recognition, they have been able to assume a more independent attitude. The more we recognize their right to existence, the greater will be their usefulness.

A tolerably recent innovation of the agencies

is the right claimed by them to ask for "Signed Statements," and the requests are complied with much oftener than might be supposed. A statement made over the signature of a dealer is not necessarily correct, and while the estimates of figures need be taken with some allowance, they are, yet, much better than the purely guess-work (in many instances unavoidable) of the reporters. Where a signed statement of the assets and liabilities is given, the only task, and a comparatively easy one, is to have it corroborated.

The idea of "Signed Statements" is a good one, and the creditor class, for whose benefit they are obtained, have a right to expect them. A mercantile report of this kind, furthermore, has a legal status. The party giving it does so for the purpose of obtaining credit on the representations made by him, and in case of a false statement, the law attaches a criminal accountability to such misrepresentations; that is, obtaining goods under false pretenses. No debtor can afford to make himself liable under this head.

The history of the Mercantile Agency shows a determined opposition to it on the part of the public, and only in the last twenty years or so has popular prejudice been removed. A little of it lurks even now in remote localities. The very nature of the institution and its inquisitorial functions naturally arouse antagonism, and, strange to say, for it is paradoxical, the free citizen of the United States is the only one on the face of the globe who tolerates it. It is a purely American institution and flourishes only on American soil. Aside from a few branch offices established in the principal European cities by Bradstreet and Dun & Co., they are not recognized, and these branches exist only for the information they can give of American houses.

Europeans do not take kindly to anything of an inquisitorial nature. The Church and State have always monopolized and claimed the right to pry into their affairs, and they graciously submit, but they are averse to any additional encroachments on their privacy.

In England, banks furnish their customers with information concerning the standing of parties in trade. A customer of a bank is privileged to make inquiry through it, and banks obtain from each other such information as may be wanted. In Europe, banking institutions are excrutiatingly exacting, and in the matter of obtaining and giving information they would naturally be very cautious and painstaking, so that reports received from this source would be quite reliable. We do not apprehend, of course, that banks are eager to lend themselves to this kind of business, and only in special cases, and as special favors to very good customers, do they perform this office.

The growth and efficiency of the Mercantile Agency in the United States, as compared with its status in other countries, is due to natural causes and more favorable conditions. Credit here is dispensed with a liberal hand, and to people very distantly removed from the sellers, but this does not signify that credits are made hap-hazard and without some knowledge of the buyer's commercial standing. And here the agency comes in as a medium between buyer and seller. In round numbers there are over 1,000,000 business firms in the United States, and the agencies furnish information of them all, and, even if incorrect in many instances, they still give us an idea of their commercial standing, where otherwise we could not even make a guess. The assistance which they render in facilitating business intercourse is, therefore, of great and unquestionable benefit.

We stated at the beginning that the mercantile agencies were the outgrowth of our credit system. It may also be added that our present widely extended credit system is largely due to the labors of the agencies, and it is no longer a disputed question that they supply a want, and are indispensable to the business public.